T0341951

Creating the Entrepreneurial Organization

Roger Cartwright

ENTERPRISE 02.10

- *The* fast track route to creating a truly entrepreneurial culture in any organization
- Covers all the critical behaviours of entrepreneurial organizations, from risk taking to growth, and from leadership to motivation
- Examples and lessons from benchmark businesses, including Microsoft, easyJet and Star Cruises
- Includes a glossary of key concepts and a comprehensive resources guide

>>EXPRESS EXEC.COM<<

essential management thinking at your fingertips

First published 2002 by
Capstone Publishing (A Wiley Company)
8 Newtec Place
Magdalen Road
Oxford OX4 1RE
United Kingdom
http://www.capstoneideas.com

CIP catalogue records for this book are available from the British Library and the US Library of Congress

ISBN 1-84112-247-5

Contents

Introduction to ExpressExec

ExpressExec is 3 million words of the latest management thinking compiled into 10 modules. Each module contains 10 individual titles forming a comprehensive resource of current business practice written by leading practitioners in their field. From brand management to balanced scorecard, ExpressExec enables you to grasp the key concepts behind each subject and implement the theory immediately. Each of the 100 titles is available in print and electronic formats.

Through the ExpressExec.com Website you will discover that you can access the complete resource in a number of ways:

» printed books or e-books;
» e-content - PDF or XML (for licensed syndication) adding value to an intranet or Internet site;
» a corporate e-learning/knowledge management solution providing a cost-effective platform for developing skills and sharing knowledge within an organization;
» bespoke delivery - tailored solutions to solve your need.

Why not visit www.expressexec.com and register for free key management briefings, a monthly newsletter and interactive skills checklists. Share your ideas about ExpressExec and your thoughts about business today.

Please contact elound@wiley-capstone.co.uk for more information.

Introduction to Creating the Entrepreneurial Organization

- Growth in organization terms is the result of the activities of those termed entrepreneurs.
- Many of the developments we take for granted today are the results of ground-breaking entrepreneurial actions by those who were at the cutting edge of the business or industry and saw ways to move forward.
- Organizational entrepreneurship is a function of the organizational life cycle, the state of the market, and the personalities within the organization.

The beginning of the nineteenth century saw the world in the midst of what has become known as the Industrial Revolution. The start of the twentieth century was a time of considerable developments in communications with the introduction of electronic means of long distance communications and the development of theories of management, and the twenty-first century opened with a huge growth in the application of ICT (information and communications technology), linking telecommunications with the use of computers. All three periods provide considerable opportunities for those organizations deemed entrepreneurial.

Entrepreneurial organizations are characterized by their willingness to take risks (albeit carefully calculated ones) and break new ground. They are dynamic, creative, and often reflect the dynamism and vision of their creator and leader in a highly visible manner.

George Bernard Shaw, quoted by the UK management guru Charles Handy in 1989, once remarked that all progress is dependent upon unreasonable people. Reasonable people adapt their behavior to the world whilst the unreasonable persist in trying to adapt the world. Therefore progress and change depend upon the unreasonable. Entrepreneurs are unreasonable because they do not accept the status quo and conventional thinking but introduce new ideas, both in terms of products and services and the way in which they are delivered. The entrepreneur and his or her organization seek out opportunities and act on them, taking a risk where necessary. Failure is accepted as a natural consequence of the entrepreneurial culture and is something to learn from, and turn to eventual profit, not something to use as a stick to beat and blame employees with. Where the entrepreneurial organization leads, more conventional organizations follow, adapting their behavior to the changed norms. However, by then the entrepreneurial organization will have moved on to new ventures. Many entrepreneurs have a low boredom threshold–not for them the building of a huge, stable organization; they leave that to others and move on to use their creativity and dynamism in other fields.

Without the entrepreneurs the nineteenth century would not have seen the growth in rail transport that so revolutionized trade and commerce, and the late twentieth and early twenty-first centuries would not have witnessed home computers and mobile telephones with the access to the global markets that they have brought via the Internet. Unless entrepreneurship is encouraged, business becomes stagnant and lacks new ideas, and whole economies can slow down. The entrepreneurial organization is a key factor in the success of every sector of business leading as it does the changes that the sector needs to make to survive and grow.

This material is designed to provide an understanding of the entrepreneurial organization by examining such organizations and providing examples of both success and failures because, as stated earlier, it is through failure as much as success that such organizations learn and grow and thus benefit all of society.

As the speed of technological and business change increases, as it has being doing since the end of World War II, so the importance of those organizations that can adapt quickly and exploit new opportunities has been greater than ever. To survive, even the most conservative of organizations are having to develop a degree of entrepreneurship. Tradition and past history count for little at a time when competitors and customers are growing ever more sophisticated and, in the case of the latter, demanding.

THE ORGANIZATIONAL LIFE CYCLE

As will be shown in the following chapters of this book, not all organizations are entrepreneurial and even those that are have not always been or always will be. Entrepreneurism is a function of certain parts of the organizational life cycle (to be introduced in Chapters 2 and 3), the state of the market, and of the personalities within the organization.

INDIVIDUAL ENTREPRENEURSHIP

This material is about the entrepreneurial organization. The attributes and skills required for the individual to become an entrepreneur are covered in a companion ExpressExec publication entitled *The Entrepreneurial Individual*. Both of these are complementary but can also be used on their own.

What is the Entrepreneurial Organization?

- Organizations are structures devised by humans to fulfill certain objectives.
- Entrepreneurism is a proactive, customer-centered, measured risk-taking method of conducting business.
- Entrepreneurial organizations take measured, carefully analyzed, and calculated risks.
- The aim of entrepreneurship is growth.
- Organizations, like humans (and products/services), undergo a life cycle.
- Certain points in the life cycle are more conducive to entrepreneurial activities than others.
- Entrepreneurial organizations still need people in them who are able to carry out the more mundane routine tasks.

Before beginning an investigation of entrepreneurism it is necessary to define what is meant by the term organization.

ORGANIZATIONS

An organization, be it a company, the administration running a town or city, the military, or even a national government, can be defined as a structure designed to fulfill a set of human objectives by maximizing the talents of its individual human and non-human components. Organizations are set up to do something–to make, to service, to govern, to transport, to defend, etc.

ENTREPRENEURISM

It is also necessary to define what is meant by entrepreneurism. In fact entrepreneurism is a number of things, not a single factor. An entrepreneurial organization is one that is concerned with growth, is proactive rather than reactive, customer focused, can assess the risks involved in a venture and then take risks that seem likely to bring sustained growth and market share, is prepared to tolerate failure, and, lastly, has a large number of its employees who share the vision and believe in the organization.

Risks

In discussing entrepreneurism it must not be thought that risk in these terms means a lack of caution. Entrepreneurial organizations (and indeed individuals) weigh risks very carefully and then after a careful analysis of all the internal and external factors may take a risk that a more conservative organization would eschew but only if the pay-off is high and the risk is not likely to endanger organizational survival. Risk is a relative term.

There are many good organizations that are not entrepreneurial. They do not take measured risks, they do not tolerate failure, and they are not populated with true believers. Nevertheless they survive but perhaps never fulfill their potential.

ORGANIZATIONAL CHANGE

Organizations can undergo a life cycle similar to that for products and indeed similar to that for human beings. Marketing experts use a concept called the product life cycle and Roger Cartwright and George Green (1997) adapted this idea when they put forward the concept of an organizational life cycle. They suggested that organizations, like products, go through a series of changes:

» birth
» adolescence
» maturity
» menopause
» decline.

They suggested that it was possible for changes at the menopausal stage resulting in decline to be averted and the organization to gain a new, albeit different, lease of life.

In the context of the entrepreneurial organization, certain points in the organizational life cycle are more in tune with entrepreneurial actions than others (Fig. 2.1).

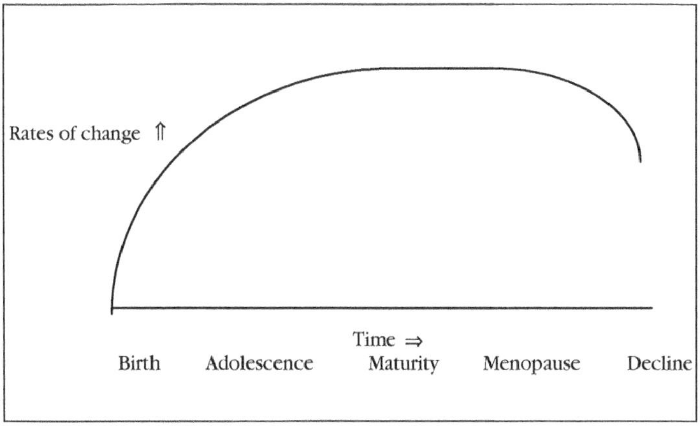

Fig. 2.1 Organizational life cycle basic model (Cartwright and Green, 1997, with permission).

Birth

At this stage a newly formed organization will be keen to gain customers and establish itself within the marketplace. As many new organizations are started by those with an entrepreneurial outlook, birth is often a time when the organization itself is entrepreneurial. The aim at the birth stage is to raise market awareness and to gain a degree of market share for the organization's products or services. There is a danger that the organization may promise more than it can deliver either in terms of quality or demand exceeding supply. A new company may be relatively naive but can well be dealing with sophisticated customers. The entrepreneur in charge of such an organization may well need people around him or her who are experienced in the day-to-day operations of an organization within the particular sector to ensure that customer demands regarding supply, quality, and after-sales service can be met. Such an entrepreneurial organization can change very rapidly but may attempt changes that are beyond its resources. Customers may demand more and more in an attempt to gain greater value for less cost and the organization may well attempt to respond with the resultant possible drain on its cash flows. An organization that wishes to survive into adolescence needs to realize which changes it can encompass and which it cannot.

Adolescence

The adolescent organization is usually gaining both in confidence and sophistication and remains entrepreneurial. As William Heinecke and Jonathon Marsh wrote in 2000, the entrepreneurial culture should be fun and adolescent organizations are renowned for both their dynamism and their sense of enjoyment (and occasional frustration) enjoyed by those associated with them. The customer base is likely to be growing and the keeping of repeat customers becomes as important as gaining new ones. The organization will be developing a history and culture and can thus be more discriminating in the changes it is prepared to introduce. It is less likely to accept demands beyond its resources. This can be a very dangerous time for the entrepreneurial organization as it may be vulnerable to take-over by more established players as Cartwright and Baird pointed out in 1999 in their study of the growth in the global cruise industry. Adolescent organizations often have cash flow problems associated with growth and a cash-rich competitor may attempt to gain control or use the cash situation to force the organization out of the market. An adolescent organization may be very vulnerable when faced with mature competitors. The acquisition of the highly successful but relatively young Princess Cruises (of Love Boat® television series fame) by the much older UK-based P&O Group in 1974 was a classic example of this.

Maturity

This is the time of greatest stability and thus a period when the organization may not want to make changes unless they are forced upon it. It is a time of the least entrepreneurial activity and there is a danger that the organization may begin to take its customers for granted and be reluctant to accept the changes they require.

Menopause

Medically, doctors tend to say of the menopause that it may cause no problems at all or at its extreme be characterized by hot flushes, tearfulness, anxiety, profound depression, inability to concentrate, inability to deal with problems, and an inability to make decisions. Biologically, menopause is a condition built into the endocrine (hormonal) system of the body and that it will occur is inevitable. Menopause is often referred to in Western society as "The Change." It is not necessarily a change for the worse. Cartwright and Green used the concept to equate a natural part of the human life cycle to that of organizations to aid understanding of organizational behavior.

It is reported that many women find that they acquire new interests after menopause and in a similar fashion many organizations develop in new and exciting ways; in fact it can become a time of renewed entrepreneurial activity.

Cartwright and Green believed that there is a menopausal stage in many organizations where, after a period of relative maturity, outside forces (the equivalent of the body's hormones) cause alterations in markets, technologies, and customer requirements. In a similar manner to hormones in the body, the organization cannot control these forces and this may bring about inability in decision making, a failure to deal with problems, organization anxiety, and depression. The organization becomes more interested in its own internal problems rather than those of its customers and any changes tend to be inwardly focused on systems and especially organizational structures rather than on the products, services, and customers. Lethargy becomes a danger. A paradoxical danger because lethargy is what will destroy the organization, and yet just when the organization needs to concentrate on its position and survival, it becomes lethargic. The main dangers are ultimate decline following a loss of customer base or else a take-over by a competitor. Indeed menopausal organizations may be at risk from predatory adolescent ones that have the energy but require the respectability of an older player in the market. Rates of change are often very low.

An organization that recognizes the menopausal stage can often take steps to rejuvenate itself and this may mean hard decisions. The aim is to become vibrant and entrepreneurial once more but the organization must ensure that the changes it makes are the ones its customers want. Often this is referred to as "the organization reinventing itself."

A model that more accurately reflects the complete organizational life cycle is shown in Fig. 2.2.

Decline

Organizations hope that they never decline but Pan Am, the US passenger shipping industry, and many retail stores that were household names have gone, some like Pan Am to reappear as smaller scale operations, others never to be heard of again; often they have been acquired by a more vibrant organization and the name has been lost. If an organization cannot compete by making the changes customers require, it will decline and die or else be swallowed up by a more successful competitor. Decline is often characterized by restructuring upon restructuring and there is a frantic attempt to deliver something that even if it does not make much money at will at least pay the wages.

Rejuvenation

Rejuvenation is akin to rebirth and thus there is the opportunity to do new things and behave differently - to act in an entrepreneurial manner.

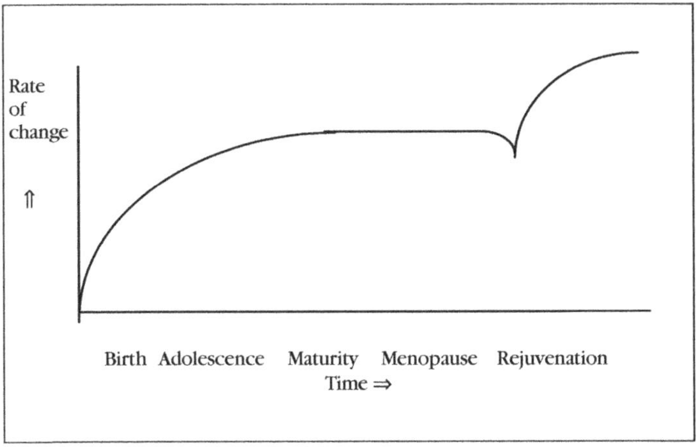

Fig. 2.2 Organizational life cycle expanded model (Cartwright and Green, 1997, with permission).

The position of an organization is in its life cycle will affect its strengths and weaknesses and make some opportunities more important than others and some threats much more dangerous than others. It is easier to be entrepreneurial at birth and adolescence and also post-menopause but only if decline is recognized and avoided.

DEVELOPING AN ENTREPRENEURIAL ORGANIZATION

Whilst many of the market aspects of the organizational life cycle are beyond the control of the organization there is much that organizational decision makers can accomplish in making the organization as entrepreneurial as possible at any stage. This should assist in producing the maximum possible growth commensurate with the situation. By the use of case studies and references this material seeks to direct decision makers in the right direction for their organization so that they will be able to take advantage of as many opportunities as possible. The concepts are applicable right across organizational sectors and know few if any geographical boundaries.

Routines

Even in the most exciting and entrepreneurial organization there will still be routine tasks that need to be carried out. Salaries and suppliers need to be paid, stock must be ordered, facilities must be cleaned and maintained, etc. Such tasks often require skills and attributes of attention to detail and a focus on what may appear trivial. As Meredith Belbin, the developer of team role theory has pointed out, successful teams (and entrepreneurial organizations tend to rely heavily on teamwork) are composed of a balance of roles, some creative, some entrepreneurial, and others concerned with routines and maintenance. In any successful entrepreneurial organization there will be those whose role is purely to deal with what appears mundane and routine. However, if the staff are not paid or the reception area is dirty then the business will suffer. These roles are just as important as the more exciting entrepreneurial ones.

KEY LEARNING POINTS

» Risks should only be taken in a measured way after careful analysis and calculation of the pay-offs and with a high chance of success.
» Risks and failure can be tolerated provided that the survival of the organization is not threatened.
» Birth, adolescence, and rejuvenation are the most conducive points of the organizational life cycle for entrepreneurial activities.
» Entrepreneurial activity can transform decline into rejuvenation.
» Entrepreneurship is not limited by geography or by organizational sectors.
» Adolescence, menopause, and decline are periods of organizational vulnerability to cash-rich predators.
» Routine tasks may be as important as entrepreneurial ones.

The Evolution of the Entrepreneurial Organization

- Entrepreneurism grew as trade became increasingly global.
- Single ventures developed into organizations, many of which were funded by investment in stocks and bonds.
- Entrepreneurs are not necessarily creative but they do understand markets and business.
- Organizations can change their culture over time; the tendency is for them to become more bureaucratic as they grow larger.
- The individual entrepreneur can be replaced by an entrepreneurial focus allowing the organization to retain a spirit of entrepreneurship.
- The customer-centered approach that characterizes the entrepreneurial organization reflects the "age" that the customer is living in.

In the previous chapter it was stated that entrepreneurial organizations are characterized by:

- a concern for growth;
- proactivity;
- customer focus;
- assessing the risks involved in a venture and then taking those measured risks that seem likely to bring sustained growth and market share;
- being prepared to tolerate failure; and
- having a large number of its employees who share the vision and believe in the organization.

A glance at any history book will show that entrepreneurism has been around for a long time as countries, organizations such as the British and Dutch East India Companies, and even individuals have sought to control and profit from trade, either free trade or trade through colonization.

Colonialism has existed since the dawn of civilization. Among the most notable colonial empires of the ancient world were those of the Egyptians, Babylonians, and Persians. The Phoenicians, who are generally acknowledged as the earliest overseas colonizers, established colonies along the shores of the Mediterranean as early as 1100 BC. Phoenician colonization was motivated principally by the desire to expand and control trade, i.e. for entrepreneurial rather than for strategic military reasons. From the eighth century BC many of the Greek city-states expanded rapidly along the coasts of the north Aegean, the Black Sea, and southern Italy. The Greeks were impelled by the need for arable land to sustain a growing population and the desire to facilitate commerce and trade. The city of Carthage, in present-day Tunisia, was founded as a Phoenician colony but eventually became an important colonial power itself attempting to control Mediterranean trade by establishing a maritime empire that included colonies in Spain and Sicily. This brought Carthage and its empire into conflict with Rome. In the Punic Wars of the second and third centuries BC the Romans defeated Carthage and laid the foundations of their huge empire, ruling over much of Europe and the Middle East in the following centuries.

In the Middle Ages, following the collapse of Roman power in the fifth century, there was little colonization. Scandinavian Vikings, however, expanded their domains considerably in the ninth and tenth centuries, establishing control over large areas of the British Isles and founding settlement colonies in Iceland and Greenland, and even Russia perhaps as far south as Kiev.

Modern European colonialism dates from the fifteenth century and lasted from about 1415 until as late as World War II. Initially Western Europe, led by Spain and Portugal, expanded in the East Indies and the Americas; in the second, Great Britain spearheaded European expansion into Asia, Africa, and the Pacific and displaced Spain and France as the major power in North America.

The Portuguese, enjoying the advantages of political stability, maritime experience, and a favorable geographic position, were the first Europeans to make their way around the southern tip of Africa to South and East Asia in the fifteenth century. They were interested primarily in dominating the growing spice trade.

By the late sixteenth century the English (Great Britain did not exist until the Act of Union between Scotland and England in 1707) and the Dutch were seriously challenging Portugal's eastern trade monopoly. The Dutch established themselves at the Cape of Good Hope, eventually drove out the Portuguese, and by 1800 controlled Java and Ceylon (now Sri Lanka). Meanwhile, the English (later British) East India Company established itself in India and formally began the conquest of the mainland in 1757.

Whilst Columbus was probably not the first European to reach North America, as it is now believed that the Vikings had done so nearly 500 years earlier, his name is still connected with the discovery of the New World. Based on information acquired during his travels, and by reading and studying charts and maps, Columbus concluded that the Earth was smaller than was previously thought, composed mostly of land and most definitely a globe and not flat. On the basis of these faulty beliefs, he decided that the riches of the East could be reached quickly by sailing west. In 1484 he submitted his theories to John II, king of Portugal, petitioning him to finance a westward crossing of the Atlantic Ocean. His proposal was rejected because of doubts about his calculations and because Portuguese ships were already rounding

Africa and were thus able to bring back spices and silks etc. albeit using what Columbus believed was an overlong route.

Soon after, Columbus moved to Spain, where his plans won the support of several influential persons, and in 1486 he secured an introduction to Isabella I, queen of Castile. In April 1492 his persistence was rewarded: Ferdinand V, king of Castile, and Queen Isabella agreed to sponsor the expedition. Columbus made a landfall in the Bahamas on October 12, 1492 and the European colonization of North America had begun. In a false belief that the Indies had been reached by sailing west from Europe the area around the Caribbean Sea is still known as the West Indies, i.e. the Indies to the west!

European colonization of the Americas was motivated by many objectives. These included the quest for gold and silver, the need for new land for agriculture, the search for freedom from religious and political persecution, and the desire to convert the indigenous peoples to Christianity. Settlement colonies were generally established rather than trading posts although, once established, these colonies traded extensively and exclusively with their respective parent nations in Europe. Spain's empire was the most prominent in the New World, spreading across much of Central and South America. The Portuguese settled mainly in Brazil (where Portuguese is still the national language). Whereas the Spanish and Portuguese tended to form mixed settlements that absorbed the indigenous populations of their territories, the British and French settlers in North America tended to form pure colonies, eliminating or displacing the previous inhabitants.

By the beginning of the 1800s the European empires had largely declined. Most of the Spanish, Portuguese, and French colonies in the Americas gained independence during and in the aftermath of the Napoleonic wars. The Dutch, too, lost their modest empire in the New World and were content to trade, often illicitly, with the colonies of other foreign powers, although the Dutch still maintained a large presence in the East Indies. The British lost their original North American colonies, which became independent in 1776, but Britain remained an important colonial power. In addition to controlling India, it retained for strategic purposes some of the foreign colonies it had occupied during the European wars, such as Canada, the Cape of Good Hope, and Ceylon. Britain's colonial empire of the late eighteenth century still forms the basis of the Commonwealth group of nations.

Later colonization followed less of a consistent pattern geographically and for the most part did not seem to be the result of a conscious desire on the part of the metropolitan powers to acquire new territory. Instead, the impetus for expansion more often came from European interests already well established on the periphery seeking the expansion of trade and increased security; for example, the Russian conquest of Central Asia was carried out largely for security reasons to support merchants, settlers, and administrators established in the local area. There was also a need for a maritime nation such as Britain to establish a chain of coaling stations around the world to service her growing stream-driven merchant fleet and navy.

The colonial powers were very active in the period between the start of the nineteenth century and the commencement of World War I when the colonization of the majority of Africa and parts of Asia and the Pacific was completed. By 1914 the British Empire was by far the largest and most diverse, but France, Belgium, Germany, Portugal, the United States, and Japan were also significant colonial powers.

The collapse of the European balance of power and successive global wars in the twentieth century signaled the demise of modern colonialism. The growth of national awareness in the colonies, the decline of European political and military influence, and the erosion of the moral justification for empire contributed to rapid decolonization after 1945. In a matter of three decades, the colonial empires, built over a number of centuries, were almost totally dismantled.

Colonization led to the beginnings of global trade. Initially trade voyages were financed by rulers and governments to supplement their coffers and to pay for military expeditions etc. The voyages of Sir Francis Drake were at the behest and for the profit of the English queen, Elizabeth I. It was not long, however, before wealthy merchants began to finance such trade, often forming syndicates to finance particular voyages and to share out the profits. Whilst the sailors took physical risks, the financial risks to the merchants were in fact small compared to the fantastic profits that could be made. As in all commercial activity the merchants were supplying a growing customer demand for luxuries and unusual items. Both on sea and land large quantities of goods (and as the slave trade grew as an unfortunate and tragic consequence) and people were moving around the globe.

An investor with money could share vicariously in the excitement of the age by putting into a trading venture and with luck would make a profit. These ventures were not like the incorporated or joint stock companies of today. At the end of each venture the syndicate would divide all of the profits and dissolve. This was a very inefficient method of managing increasingly large commercial ventures and thus organizations (companies) were set up to exist beyond a particular venture. Many of these companies sought investment not just from wealthy private benefactors but also from a growing middle class. Unfortunately the early stock market was even more volatile than it is today and after the South Sea Bubble fiasco of 1720 the British government began to regulate trade and its financial aspects more rigorously.

The South Sea Bubble plan was devised by Robert Harley, Earl of Oxford, in 1711, for paying off Great Britain's national debt. Under the plan, the debt was assumed by merchants to whom the government guaranteed for a certain period annual payments equal to $3 million. This sum, amounting to 6% interest, was to be obtained from duties on imports from certain areas. The monopoly held by sections of British trade in the South Seas and South America was given to these merchants, incorporated as the South Sea Company, and extravagant ideas of the riches of South America were fostered to attract investors. In the spring of 1720 the company offered to assume practically the whole national debt, at that time equal to more than $150 million. Companies of all kinds were floated to take advantage of the public interest in obtaining South Sea Company stock. Speculation soon carried stock to 10 times its nominal value despite there being no earnings at the time. The chairman and some directors sold out, the bubble burst, and the stock collapsed. Thousands of stockholders were ruined. Parliamentary investigation revealed complicity by some company officials and other public notables including members of the royal court of George I. However, a political crisis was averted through the efforts of Sir Robert Walpole, who at that time was serving as the Chancellor of the Exchequer and later became the first person to hold a post equated with that of the present-day UK prime minister. Only about one-third of the original capital was recovered for the stockholders.

Despite this failure the public soon took to this form of investment and organizations were able to raise money through ownership rather than borrowing. This greatly aided those with ideas and who could convince investors to take a modest risk with them. Investors by their weight of numbers were spreading individual risk and thus facilitating entrepreneurship.

THE GROWTH OF MODERN ORGANIZATIONS

Many of those who started new organizations were not inventors or mariners or craftspeople. Their skills lay in seeing opportunities and raising finance. These were the entrepreneurs. It has become apparent over the years that commercial progress needs not only creativity but also the vision and financial skills of the entrepreneur. Many of the most famous inventors such as the Wright brothers (aircraft), Stephenson (railways), Sinclair in the UK (consumer electronics) were not good business people. What people like them needed was a partnership with an entrepreneur and a structure within which to operate. That structure becomes the organization and it is in the nature of organizations that the successful ones will outlive their creative and entrepreneurial founders.

In the middle of the nineteenth Century the German sociologist Max Weber termed the phrase bureaucracy as a method of operation for large organizations. Weber and later Fayol in Belgium saw the need for structure and rules in the operation of organizations that were rapidly increasing in size. The Industrial Revolution and the ability of workers to live at increasing distances from their place of employment due to the efficiency of new transport systems (trains, streetcars, etc.) had led to organizations of hundreds and thousands of workers whereas earlier organizations had been smaller. In earlier times the owner was usually the manager and knew most workers personally. Larger organizations need a much more structured approach. Bureaucracy at the time was considered the answer although it is now a term of derision. Nevertheless writers on organizational culture such as Charles Handy in the UK have noted that the culture of organizations tends to become more rule bound and bureaucratic as the organization becomes older and more mature. Unfortunately the more bureaucratic an organization is the more it tends to behave in a less than entrepreneurial manner. Bureaucracy and entrepreneurship do not sit well together.

Handy has defined bureaucratic organizations as role cultures (depicted by a Greek Temple – highly stable but slow to change) in contrast with the spider's web of a power or club culture that is more reflective of many entrepreneurial organizations. At the center of the web was (and in new organizations is) the individual entrepreneur in whom much of the organization power and ultimate decision making are invested. This does not mean, however, that there must be an individual entrepreneur for an organization to be entrepreneurial. It is true that the individuals in charge of the organization must be sympathetic to entrepreneurial ideals but it is possible for the individual entrepreneur to be replaced by an entrepreneurial focus such as supreme customer care. British Airways before its privatization in the 1980s was a highly bureaucratic organization exhibiting all the features of a typical role culture. After privatization and the introduction of dynamic new management it became a watchword for innovation and a customer-centered approach to the extent that in the early 1990s it was one of the few airlines that was able to grow through being consistently profitable.

Throughout the latter nineteenth and early twentieth centuries entrepreneurial organizations, headed initially by individual entrepreneurs but later driven by the vision those individuals had bequeathed to the organization, built railroads, opened department stores, took to the skies, crossed the oceans, developed household and entertainment goods, and produced new medicines. This process still goes on both in traditional industries and in the newer dot com sectors that became an important part of the late 1990s and early twenty-first century. Organizations with drive, customer focus, vision, and a careful analysis of risk coupled with the willingness to tolerate a degree of failure are the ones that grow. Whether they can keep that culture for ever is debatable, but if they are aware of the dangers of losing their focus and becoming too staid and bureaucratic they can reinvent themselves to remain at the forefront of their particular sector, as will be shown in the succeeding chapters of this book. Where The Union Pacific Railroad in the United States and the Great Western Railway in the UK, Cunard and J P Morgan's shipping empire, and John Wannamaker and Isador Strauss (US department store entrepreneurs) led, Amazon.com, Sony, Disney, Bodyshop, and Virgin followed as their modern successors seeking growth and delighting customers.

THE AGES OF ENTREPRENEURSHIP

It has become the norm to consider much of history in terms of "revolutions" or ages; for example, the agricultural and industrial revolutions/ages. These ages are linked to the type of entrepreneurship prevalent at the time.

Prior to about 1750 there was the exploration age where entrepreneurship was mainly connected with the mechanics of trade and exchange. There followed a revolution in agriculture and at this time many entrepreneurs became involved with the development of new forms of husbandry. From the 1800s onwards came the Industrial Revolution and entrepreneurial activity was often directed at manufacturing and transportation. The industrial age lasted well into the second half of the twentieth century and is still a major feature of many economies, but in much of the developed world the service age followed by the current information age has succeeded it as the trend for entrepreneurship. Larry Farrell (see Chapter 8) has described the nineteenth century as the industrial age, the twentieth as the managerial age, and the twenty-first as the entrepreneurial age. In doing so Farrell was seeking to distinguish between managerial and entrepreneurial organizations - a useful distinction to make as he believes that management is a function of the more mature end of the organizational life cycle whilst entrepreneurship as discussed in the previous chapter occurs during birth and adolescence. Nevertheless it must not be thought that entrepreneurship is a recent phenomenon; as discussed earlier it has been around since trade began. Entrepreneurship is a function of what is happening in the wider society. One of the key characteristics of the entrepreneurial organization is a customer-centered approach and thus the organization must reflect in its products and services the needs and wants of its customers and these in turn reflect the age the customer is living in.

These ages are represented by the time line shown in Fig. 3.1.

KEY LEARNING POINTS

- Entrepreneurship has existed since humans began to trade with each other.

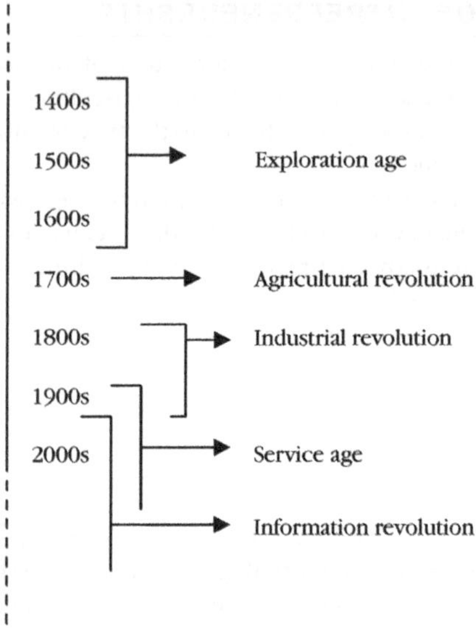

Fig. 3.1 Time line.

- It is not necessary to be a creative inventor to be entrepreneurial.
- Bureaucracy stifles entrepreneurship.
- Organizations can retain an entrepreneurial culture even when the original entrepreneur has moved on.
- It is possible for organizations to reinvent themselves to remain entrepreneurial.

The E-Dimension

- Organizations and e-commerce fall into the following categories: suppliers of hardware/software/consumables, existing organizations using the Net as an adjunct to their business, and those founded to use the Net.
- Using e-commerce and the Internet increases the customer base.
- Markets can undergo segment shift; the e-commerce market is no different and now includes all ages and both business and domestic users.
- Take-up of e-commerce has been slower than many of those founding dot com companies anticipated.
- Security remains an issue in e-commerce.

The Internet and e-commerce have had a dual effect on the concept of the entrepreneurial organization. Firstly there have been those companies that have been formed or have moved into supplying the e-commerce and computer markets, e.g. Microsoft and Apple, and there have been others who have been formed or have altered their operations to avail themselves of the new advantages offered by e-commerce and the Internet e.g. easyJet (see later in this chapter and Chapter 7) and Amazon.com. In many ways the former have driven the Internet as we see it today whilst the latter have been the organizations that have exploited the advantages the Net has offered to them.

SUPPLIERS TO THE INTERNET

Materials

From the days of the original calculating machines through to modern computers, entrepreneurial organizations have been quick to supply the materials necessary to make the most effective use of them. Whilst creative geniuses such as Charles Babbage (the inventor of the mechanical counting machine) through to Clive Sinclair in the UK, who pioneered early home computers, have moved the technology forward, such developments have also needed more mundane supporting materials: paper rolls, punched cards, floppy disks, CD-ROMs, etc. 3M (Minnesota Mining & Manufacturing) formed by a group of six Minnesota miners facing bankruptcy due to the failure of their gravel pit operation in 1906 has moved from abrasives to adhesive tape and then into the original five inch floppy disks. The company saw a market that was expanding and was within its competence to enter and did so with success. Sharp, Toshiba, Hewlett Packard are just some of the organizations that supply both hardware and the all-important consumables to support it.

The supply of necessary support materials provides good potential for the entrepreneurial organization. If it has carried out its market analysis correctly there will be a good understanding of what the customers for the hardware products are likely to need. Organizations such as Avery Dennison, well known in the global office supplies market, have adapted their product range to include diskette, CD and envelope labels to a degree that Microsoft Word® includes templates for

Avery labels amongst others as standard. Generic suppliers, i.e. those wholesalers and retailers who produce own-brand products, have also tapped the huge computer consumables market with paper, diskettes, etc., cheaper than branded products but still of high quality.

As the computer market has expanded from the commercial into the domestic sectors those able to produce software, of which Microsoft is probably the best-known name all over the world (having such a supposed monopoly as to cause legal action by the US government), and games have prospered. To be entrepreneurial in this field means keeping a careful watch on the increasing capability of the hardware and being able to supply faster and better programs and games almost at the point of introduction of a hardware development. This point is emphasized when considering the success of Microsoft in Chapter 7.

Even such a mundane item as paper, once thought to be obsolete due to the concept of the paperless office, is still required for computers. Ease of printing and a desire for the security of a hard copy has provided opportunities for those entrepreneurial organizations that can produce paper products to suit computer users.

The linking of telephone and video technology with microprocessor developments has provided opportunities for PC-top video conferencing, a huge growth in digital still and video cameras, and ever sophisticated mobile telephones. That care must be taken was shown in 2001 when British Telecom (BT) found that it needed to raise large sums of money by splitting up the business having spent a great deal on buying UK mobile telephone licenses from the government to support the next generation of mobile telephones. Despite the fact that by 2001 over 50% of the UK population had a mobile telephone BT's expenditure was in fact too high.

SEGMENT SHIFT

The concept of what might be called segment shifting is one used frequently by entrepreneurial organizations. It is the movement of a product from one market to another. It has occurred very successfully in the ICT area but is also seen in other industries. It may occur geographically, sectorally, or demographically. The following examples will illustrate the point.

Geographically

It is not unusual for motor vehicle and motor cycle manufacturers to market a product in a range of countries moving from one to another as required or to move a whole plant from country to country. The Honda 50 motorcycle was marketed first in Japan, then the United States, then Europe. When the product ceased to sell in large numbers in Europe the marketing switched to India, where the model was regarded as very sophisticated, and latterly to China.

With ICT, products tend to be released in the developed world simultaneously but there are still regions where last year's product may be acceptable and an entrepreneurial organization can gain quick market penetration by seeking these markets and supplying them. As the products will probably have been discounted heavily in the original market due to their perceived "datedness" they may be acquired quite inexpensively.

Sectorally

In the early 1980s the facsimile (fax) machine appeared, almost overnight, within offices in Japan, the United States, and Europe.

By the early 1990s there were few if any organizations in the developed world that did not possess a number of fax machines. In marketing terms this was a saturated market with new sales only likely to come from the replacement of older machines as there were few new business customers. However, there was a domestic market that could be tapped using combined telephone/facsimile machines based on the benefit of being able to send documents quickly and cheaply.

The computer market (famously reported in the early days by an IBM executive to have only the capacity for just six mainframe machines world-wide) has moved from a purely business/organization market to a thriving domestic one, especially following the introduction of small, powerful desktop and laptop machines generically known as PCs (personal computers; although the term was originally an IBM brand it is now used generically). As computers appear to be obsolete before being removed from the box, both these markets have good potential for follow-up sales and repeat business. In the domestic market the PC is used for many non-business purposes, e.g. games playing and personal communication.

Demographically

The third type of segment shift is across age or social groups. Products that were initially sold to a particular group may well be marketed later to a different audience. Mobile communications were originally taken up by business people but the market segment has expanded and shifted to include the young and many women not in work. This has been accomplished by stressing the benefits of keeping in touch with peers to the former and safety aspects to many of the latter. PCs, once marketed at those in business, were again later marketed at the young as a game's product and at many parents as an educational aid.

ISPS AND SEARCH ENGINES

The Internet began with the linking together of a series of computers in the US DARPA (Defense Agency Research Projects Administration) to form what became known in 1969 as ARPAnet, designed to protect military communications in the event of a nuclear attack - a very real fear in the political climate of the time. The system used three university hosts in California and one in Utah. Later in the 1970s the US academic community set up a purely civilian network funded by the NSF (National Science Foundation) which linked an increasing number of US and foreign universities via NSFnet to run alongside ARPAnet. For the first time academics and researchers could communicate text via a new medium of electronic mail, rapidly contracted to e-mail.

As students who had used e-mail began to take up positions within the private sector they took the technology with them and it was not long before large commercial organizations in the United States, beginning with computer companies such as IBM and Hewlett Packard, began to talk to each other via e-mail linking their systems to the NSFnet.

In 1993 Marc Andersen and his group at the University of Illinois introduced the first Web browser software (Mosaic), a software application for the UNIX® operating system, but later adapted for Apple Macintosh and Microsoft Windows®. NSFnet gradually became less relevant and the commercial world saw the birth of ISPs (Internet service providers - see later in this section) so that by the middle of the 1990s organizations in both the public and private sectors were not only using e-mail but beginning to design and post their own Web pages. The WWW (World Wide Web) had been born.

To be effective the Internet required a means of linking the growing number of users to the Web and effective methods of finding the material required on a web that seems to be growing exponentially.

ISPs are the link between the user and the Web. Whilst large organizations may have their own servers and access the vast majority of users are dependent upon a commercial organization to manage the link and this has been a fruitful area for entrepreneurial organizations. As organizations and individuals have become more dependent upon the Internet (some of the latter may be psychologically addicted!) so they must use an ISP. The best known is probably AOL (America on Line) operating not just in the United States but on a global basis. There are, however, many others, some local, some regional, and many national, e.g. Freeserve and Supranet in the UK. AOL is linked to Time Warner and has constantly upgraded its product showing that even a huge organization can be entrepreneurial. At the time of writing the latest version was AOL 6.0.

WEB PAGE DESIGN

Another ICT-related area where individual entrepreneurs and small entrepreneurial organizations have found a niche is in the design, hosting, and updating of Web pages. There is hardly an organization in the world that does not have its own Website and the use of such sites has developed to include sites for individuals using them for both advertising and purely personal reasons.

Whilst individuals may be able to maintain their own site, for organizations a Website may perform the same functions as a reception or front desk - it is the first point of contact for customers and potential customers. It is therefore important that a professional and positive image is presented and this may require the use of a specialist organization to design and maintain the site - a role for an entrepreneurial organization that has seen the potential of Websites and acquired the technical expertise to work in this area.

USERS OF THE INTERNET

Organizations using the Internet can be divided into two broad categories.

» Those that use the Internet as a supplement to their business.
» Those that were founded in order to use the Internet.

The Internet as a supplement to their business

Any organization with a Website is included in the first category, i.e. the vast majority of the world's organizations. In the main they existed before the Net and have used it to supplement their advertising etc. Many are moving into e-commerce as more and more customers go online and payment systems are made increasingly more secure. easyJet - the best-practice case at the end of this chapter and described in more detail in Chapter 7 - is an example of an entrepreneurial organization that has used the Net to gain its market position.

Those organizations that were entrepreneurial in their approach to the Net and set up sites at the early stages have found that they have been brought into contact with a much wider customer base.

Founded to use the Internet

Many of the dot com companies of the late 1990s and early twenty-first century were founded because the Internet had reached the stage that it had. The concept of doing all business online with the subsequent reduction in premises costs etc. was only possible as more and more people put themselves online. Much money was made (and lost) trading in the stocks of these early companies, as it was not so easy as was perhaps initially imagined for them to get into profit. There is still resistance to e-commerce due to worries about security and also because many people actually enjoy browsing in retail outlets. Shopping appears to be a social as well as a commercial activity.

Nevertheless some well-known names have emerged, of which Amazon.com is probably one of the best known, selling books and music on an increasingly global basis and dealing solely over the Internet and offering both value for money and high quality service.

Much travel is also booked online and there is no doubt that well-financed organizations that can weather the initial outlays are in with a very good chance of survival as the take-up of e-commerce increases.

Amazon.com features as a case study in Chapter 7.

Many of these organizations were founded by individual entrepreneurs who perceived that e-commerce would grow. Many of them over-anticipated the growth rate but e-commerce is here to stay and the organizations founded by these individuals will need to remain entrepreneurial if they are to stay at the forefront of the e-commerce market.

BEST PRACTICE

easyJet

easyJet (see Chapter 7 for more details), a company that commenced operations in November 1995, is one of Europe's leading low cost airlines. Since its first flight in November 1995, the company has grown from operating just two routes from Luton to Glasgow and Edinburgh, served by two Boeing 737 aircraft, to an airline offering 35 routes from 16 European airports and flying 21 737-series aircraft. During the financial year to September 30, 2000, the company reported pre-tax profits of £22 million on a turnover of £263 million and carried 5.6 million passengers.

easyJet was founded by Stelios Haji-Ioannou, who owns a majority of the shareholding and who also controls other separate easyGroup companies such as easyEverything, easyRentacar, and easyValue. The airline's headquarters is at Luton Airport to the north of London.

The Internet plays a vital part in the easyJet business and has proved crucially critical to the success of the business. As a low cost operation, controlling the cost of doing business is obviously highly important to the airline's ability to be competitive by offering low fares. The Internet provides the most cost-effective distribution channel available and easyJet has pursued its strategy of encouraging passengers to book their seats online with vigor. easyJet's main routes involve English-, French-, and Spanish-speaking destinations and thus their Website (see Chapter 9) is accessible in the three languages. easyJet has provided a series of incentives for customers to book via the Internet. Passengers booking online receive a discount of £2.50 ($4) for each leg of a journey. easyJet first pioneered the concept of offering a discount to Internet customers, an initiative that has been widely copied by an increasing number of competitors. To remain competitive easyJet is determined to offer a higher permanent level of discount than that offered by any other airline.

Any easyJet promotions are exclusive to the Internet, so that customers must book online if they wish to take advantage of discounted fares.

If customers wish to book seats more than a month in advance of the departure date of the flight, they can only do so by booking online. As fares generally increase as the departure dates gets closer, this means that the best fares are first available to those who book via the Internet.

For those not online, easyJet also operates a growing number of town and city center cyber-outlets allowing customers to drop in and use the Internet.

Since easyJet started selling seats via the Internet in April 1998, the airline has enjoyed dramatic growth in its online sales. The airline reached one million seats sold via the Internet in October 1999, and celebrated this important landmark by giving that lucky passenger unlimited free flights for a whole year. Five months later in March 2000, easyJet reached two million seats, and it only took another three months after that to reach the three million seat mark, indicating a huge acceleration in the growth of online sales. easyJet has now sold more than seven million seats online. The proportion of all sales made online has also shown impressive growth. easyJet now sells over 85% of its seats online every week, which is a higher percentage than any other airline, reinforcing the airline's stated advertising position as the "Web's favorite airline" - a parody on British Airway's claim to be the "world's favorite airline."

KEY LEARNING POINTS

- Customers are still concerned about security for e-commerce.
- Organizations supplying mundane items to support technological developments can still be entrepreneurial by anticipating those developments and being able to meet customer needs.
- E-commerce can be an adjunct to an existing business as well as the reason for founding a new one.
- New markets can be developed by analyzing the entrepreneurial potential for segment shift.

The Global Dimension of the Entrepreneurial Organization

Entrepreneurism is concerned with growing the organization in a proactive manner.

- » The Internet has begun to allow globalization of customers without the need for globalization of facilities, especially for service suppliers, and this means that more and more organizations including smaller ones can benefit from a global marketplace.
- » In order to penetrate global markets the entrepreneurial organization has to carry out careful research and analysis of the requirements and culture of those markets
- » The SPECTACLES analysis covers the main external factors that need to be included in the analysis
- » SPECTACLES stands for Social, Political, Economic, Cultural, Technological, Aesthetic, Customer, Legal, Environmental, and Sectoral.
- » A SWOT analysis is an analysis looking firstly at the strengths and weaknesses of the organization (internal) then at the threats

and opportunities facing the organization from the environment (external).

» The strengths of an organization are those things it does particularly well, especially when viewed against the operations of its competitors, whereas its weaknesses are areas in which it is less strong than the competition.
» Opportunities are those external factors where the organization can use its strengths to outclass the competition and threats are those factors from the external environment from which the organization may suffer because of its weaknesses.
» The aim should always be for strategies that build on strengths, minimize weaknesses, exploit opportunities, and defend against threats.
» An entrepreneurial organization will analyze the culture to find out what needs changing

Entrepreneurism is concerned with growing the organization in a proactive manner. There are four main ways in which an organization can grow.

» Increase the size of a current market for its current products.
» Find new markets for its current products.
» Diversify into new products.
» Acquire another organization and its product/service range and customers.

These growth methods were alluded to in the concept of segment shift introduced in the last chapter. The second and third methods often involve the organization expanding into new geographical areas. The introduction of modern transport and communication systems have simplified the globalization process, as has national membership of economic combinations such as the EU (European Union) and NAFTA (North American Free Trade Agreement).

There has also been a growing trend to employ the fourth method and acquire an organization in another area. In the 1970s the long-established UK shipping company P&O (Peninsular and Oriental Steam Navigation Company) wanted to expand into the rapidly developing US cruise industry. Unfortunately, although well known in the UK, India, and Australia the name of P&O was unknown to US customers and P&O's first attempts to set up an operation in the Caribbean and Mexican waters using the purpose-built cruise ship *Spirit of London* were not very successful. However, in 1974 P&O acquired the small but highly successful Princess Cruises founded by the US entrepreneur Stanley B. McDonald and based in Los Angeles. P&O kept the Princess brand name and this provided the base for the highly successful Princess operation by P&O, a number of the ships starring in the successful US Love Boat® television series later shown on UK television. The brand was further strengthened in 1988 when P&O, through Princess (operating as a US registered company) bought the Italian cruise company Sitmar that also had an extensive US operation. P&O has continued the Princess brand and even in 2001 the two main arms of the company's cruise business (it is the third biggest global player) are P&O Cruises operating for a predominantly UK market base and Princess Cruises for North American customers. Ships and officers are transferred between the two fleets and many UK customers also use Princess. Ships fly the same houseflag and all have a P&O logo on the side.

For more and more organizations growth requires a move into globalization. The Internet (see previous chapter) has begun to allow globalization of customers without the need for globalization of facilities, especially for service suppliers, and this means that more and more organizations including smaller ones can benefit from a global marketplace.

GOING GLOBAL - WHAT THE ENTREPRENEURIAL ORGANIZATION NEEDS TO DO

A successful entrepreneurial organization is likely to have a good product/service range and a reputation in its own home market. Such a reputation may well not transfer into other, more global markets. In order to penetrate global markets the entrepreneurial organization has to carry out careful research and analysis of the requirements and culture of those markets. The importance of culture is covered in considerable detail in *Managing Diversity* - also available as part of the ExpressExec series - and information on this topic is summarized later in this chapter.

The two analyses that the organization must carry out consider the external environment and the opportunities and threats that it can offer to the organization and secondly the strengths and weaknesses of the organization itself and how it can exploit opportunities and minimize threats.

THE SPECTACLES ANALYSIS

The SPECTACLES analysis has grown out of the traditional PEST (Political, Economic, Social, Technological) analysis. The author considered that additional components have become necessary to cope with an increasingly more complex business and social environment and published the concept of the SPECTACLES analysis in *Mastering the Business Environment* (Cartwright, 2001). The following sections are designed to act as an introduction to those components and to show the interrelationships between them.

Not only do each of the components of the analysis impact upon the organization; but also they impact upon each other as will be shown in the final part of this section.

The SPECTACLES acronym stands for Social, Political, Economic, Cultural, Technological, Aesthetic, Customer, Legal, Environmental, and Sectoral.

Social analysis

Sociology is the study of the organization and functioning of human societies. Most people live and work in close proximity to other human beings who they rely on for certain services and products. It is these relationships that form society.

The social analysis component of SPECTACLES is concerned with examining the changes in the societies with which the organization interfaces and what trends within those societies are likely to have implications for the organization. Included within this part of the analysis is a consideration of the phenomenon known as consumerism, a concept that can also be used as part of the customer analysis and the role of the media in communicating with society and influencing societal views and changes. The recent trends in the priority accorded to green/environmental issues are considered so important as to merit a section of the SPECTACLES analysis to themselves, although it must be noted that it is society itself that has raised these issues as a priority and thus the growth of green issues is a rightful part of the social analysis; the addressing of those issues forms part of the environmental analysis.

The social analysis also includes a consideration of the demographic changes (size, age, etc., of populations) which may impact upon an organization. Anticipating demographic changes can give an entrepreneurial organization a considerable competitive advantage as it may provide an indication of potential growing or declining markets. For an interesting explanation of demography you are advised to consult *Boom, Bust and Echo* by David K. Foot and Daniel Stoffman, 1996 (see Chapter 9).

Political analysis

Politics is the art and science of government. The citizens of any country are normally subject to a complex series of governmental layers. In Scotland the lowest level of government may be a Community Council, followed by a District Council, the Scottish Parliament and the UK Parliament at Westminster. As the UK is a member of the EU, Scots as UK citizens are also governed to an extent by the European Parliament. In the United States there are local laws, state law, and federal law as defined by the US Constitution.

Each layer of government has its own responsibilities and normally some form of revenue raising. As the various layers may well be controlled by political parties and groupings with differing agendas and philosophies, this can make any analysis by an organization quite complex and time sensitive as politicians tend to change their message as time progresses.

Governments produce legislation and legal issues comprise a separate part of the analysis. The political analysis is concerned with those external policy developments that concern the organization. As even the smallest organizations begin to trade globally, then it is not enough to consider indigenous political policies but also to have due regard for policies in the national regions of customers and suppliers.

Economic analysis

All organizations depend on sources of finance. Economics is always the source of much debate and the subject of countless books.

Money does make the world go around but it must be stressed that there are considerable interrelationships between political and economic factors. Governments have a vested interest in managing their economies and some may be much more interventionist in the economic field than others.

The economic analysis considers such factors as interest rates, exchange rates, wage levels, oil price, etc.

Cultural analysis

Much human and therefore organizational behavior can be traced back to culture. There are distinct types of organizational culture each of which needs to inter-react with organizations displaying different cultures. An understanding of the culture of suppliers, customers, and competitors forms an important part of the analysis of the environment.

There are also national cultures and as the world of business becomes increasingly global in nature then organizations need to take much more cognizance of the cultures they will encounter. As will be demonstrated good products can fail because those supplying them have not carried out a sufficiently in-depth analysis of the culture of the target market.

Technological analysis

It almost seems as if last year's technological miracle is this year's major best-seller.

The development of the use of computers, from purely scientific through business and then domestic markets, receives consideration followed by the implications of the Internet and e-commerce (see previous chapter), developments that affect nearly every organization world-wide.

Aesthetic analysis

Modern technology allows organizations to produce even the most mundane products and services at very high levels. Quality is becoming almost a given. In such an environment those involved externally with an organization, especially customers and potential customers, become more and more influenced by the intangibles that surround product and service delivery.

The aesthetic analysis considers the way in which those in the external environment respond to organizational image and design - design of products, packaging design, and even building design. In a link to culture it is a fact that many organizations from the Far East would not consider the design of a new building without the assistance of a Feng Shui consultant, so important is this aspect of culture.

Customer analysis

Every organization, no matter what its type or products/services, has customers. Indeed customers are the most important stakeholders of any organization. No customers eventually equals no organization - this is a universal, global rule!

Organizations need to analyze the needs of current and, most importantly, potential customers, especially those from other than the original home market. The culture etc. of these customers may be a very important feature for the organization to analyze. In the early days of television advertising many US organizations believed that they could show their US advertisements on UK television as the two nations spoke the same language. However, the cultural norms of UK customers are slightly different to those from the United States and unless allowance was made for this, purely US advertisements were not well received with a resulting failure of market penetration.

Legal analysis

All organizations need to be aware and take account of the law in those areas where they operate. Each national jurisdiction has its own set of laws and whilst many of them may be based on the same principles there will be national and even local differences as seen between the states making up the United States of America.

Whilst a detailed analysis of legal aspects in the external environment is rightly a subject for specialist lawyers, it is important that all those involved in carrying out an analysis of the external environment are aware of current legal practices and proposed legislative changes in those geographic areas within which the organization operates and that may impact upon the organization.

Environmental analysis

One of the major movements of the late twentieth century was that of environmentalism. No longer can organizations ignore the environmental implications of their actions and the effects these may have on waste disposal, pollution, biodiversity, etc. Western organizations were once notorious for ignoring the environmental impact on many of the less developed regions in which they operated. No longer is this the case, thankfully.

An environmental analysis is rightly accorded its own section in considerations of the factors affecting an organization. Indeed an environmental impact analysis may well be a condition of planning permission or funding for new projects.

Sectoral analysis

The final component of the SPECTACLES analysis concerns other organizations operating in similar markets. This includes collaborators and competitors. The actions of both of these can have a dramatic effect on an organization.

Analysis of the competition (and collaborators) includes looking at their strengths and weaknesses plus analyzing the competitive forces that are operating within the marketplace, especially where the organization is expanding into a new market and may encounter competition from more established players.

LINKS

The 10 components of the SPECTACLES analysis plus the organization itself provide for no fewer than 55 possible interactions (the number of pathways that join 11 points together). These links are important, as no component in the analysis should be considered in isolation - they all operate together.

From the SPECTACLES analysis, the opportunities and threats for a particular part of the global marketplace can be assessed and fed into a SWOT analysis.

SWOT

A SWOT (Strengths, Weaknesses, Opportunities and Threats) analysis is a common component of organizational planning and should follow the SPECTACLES analysis.

A SWOT analysis is a two-part analysis: the first part looks at the strengths and weaknesses of the organization and is thus an internal analysis, and the second part considers the threats and opportunities facing the organization from the external environment which are derived from the external analyses (see SPECTACLES above).

The strengths of an organization are those things it does particularly well, especially when viewed against the operations of its competitors, whereas its weaknesses are areas in which it is less strong than the competition.

Opportunities are those external factors where the organization can use its strengths to outclass the competition and threats are those factors from the external environment from which the organization may suffer because of its weaknesses.

The aim should always be to aim for strategies that build on strengths, minimize weaknesses, exploit opportunities, and defend against threats.

A SWOT analysis is usually displayed as a quadrant, as shown in Fig. 5.1.

Strengths	Weaknesses
Opportunities	Threats

Fig. 5.1 SWOT analysis.

There is no reason why items should appear in more than one quadrant. The large size of an organization may be seen as a strength when it comes to economies of scale but as a weakness in respect of communications. It is perfectly legitimate to place it in both quadrants.

To achieve maximum effect, a SWOT analysis should be carried out at a minimum on an annual basis and always when considering moving into a new market. It is best done as a group activity involving people from across the organization and at differing positions within the hierarchy. Different views may thus be represented. In large organizations it is not unusual for individual departments, sections, etc., to complete their own SWOT analysis on their part of the operation. When this is dome what one part of the organization may see as a strength may be regarded as a weakness by another; again this is perfectly legitimate if it aids discussion. Different views of the same issue can produce different perceptions.

It must be stressed that there is no point in undertaking an analysis of strengths and weaknesses, i.e. an internal analysis without then going on to link that analysis to one of the external opportunities and threats.

CULTURE

Culture can be defined as "the way things are done around here." Culture is, in effect, the outward manifestation of a group's values, attitudes, and beliefs. It is very easy to inadvertently produce a dissonance between the culture of an incoming organization and the indigenous culture. Workers such as Fons Trompenaars, Richard D. Lewis, and Philip R. Harris/Robert T. Moran have produced useful guides and concepts for organizations beginning to deal with new cultures. How an organization does something in Boston (MA) may need to be different to the way it does it in Boston (Lincolnshire). Operational and personnel policies in Bangalore (India) may need to be amended if the organization sets up in Brazil etc.

An entrepreneurial organization will analyze the culture to find out what needs changing - even the name of the product. The VW Golf in Europe has been branded as the Rabbit in the United States. Would Europeans buy a car branded as the Rabbit?

BEST PRACTICE

Nokia

Finland, a small northern European country with a fair proportion of its territory north of the Arctic Circle, is home to one of the major exponents of global entrepreneurship - Nokia.

From its founding in 1865, Nokia was in the communications business as a manufacturer of paper and later with the founding of the Finnish Rubber Works at the turn of the nineteenth century the company moved into the production of rubber-based products.

An electronics department was set up at the Finnish Cable Works in 1960, an electronics department was formed, and this paved the way for a new era in telecommunications. Nokia Corporation was formed in 1967 by the merger of Nokia Company - the original papermaking business - with the Finnish Rubber Works and Finnish Cable Works. It was this development that led the way to Nokia's current position in the mobile telephone market.

As the company history states, Nokia has always tried to blend aesthetics with practicality (an important part of the SPECTACLES analysis introduced earlier in this chapter). Whilst the idea of brightly colored, coordinated mobile telephones with interchangeable fronts may be recent, Nokia was producing rubber boots in bright colors some time ago as part of its rubber products operation. The same concepts apply - what does the customer want?

Nokia has been at the forefront of mobile telephone developments, researching the area long before products were on sale to the public - a typical entrepreneurial organization approach.

Where Nokia has been exceptionally successful for a company from a small country has been in its global penetration. There are few major regions in the world without a Nokia indigenous operation, e.g. Nokia Austria, Nokia UK, Nokia Brazil, etc. By making itself synonymous with the country the organization appears indigenous and thus engenders loyalty from the local customers.

Nokia's stated values are those that have a great deal of commonality with most cultures and this aids globalization as it lessens the chance of cultural dissonance. The Nokia values are:

» customer satisfaction
» respect for the individual
» achievement
» continuous learning.

These are of course the very values that distinguish entrepreneurial organizations.

Nokia says that it articulates these values through its watchwords of:

» innovation and design
» experience
» user-friendliness
» reliable solutions
» customer satisfaction.

Nokia knows its customers, wherever the customer might be, and that has assisted it in producing excellent results for its shareholders as shown below in the Nokia figures for 2000 (source Nokia Website):

» Nokia's net sales totaled & euro: 0.4 billion ($27.0 billion).
» Nokia employ over 60,000 people.
» Production locations in 10 countries.
» Research and development in 15 countries.
» Sales to over 130 countries.
» Part of the reason for Nokia's success was the appointment of Jorma Ollila as Nokia group president and CEO in 1992 (Ollila having joined the company as a vice-president in 1985).
» As Marquardt and Berger (2000) have written, Ollila is a person with vision and no organization can be entrepreneurial without vision.

KEY LEARNING POINTS

Organizations grow in one of four ways. They can:

» increase the size of a current market for their current products;
» find new markets for their current products;
» diversify into new products; and
» acquire another organization and its product/service range and customers.

» Organizations need to analyze both the internal and external environments in order to use their strengths to exploit opportunities and to defend against threats. They also need to know their own weaknesses.
» Entrepreneurial organizations entering a global market will ensure that they have researched the culture of that market. Organizations should adapt to customers, not customers to organizations.
» ICT such as the Internet means that globalization is a possibility for small as well as large organizations.

The State of the Art of Organizational Entrepreneurship

- Three types of organization are always in competition:
  1 entrepreneurial organizations;
  2 organizations that were once entrepreneurial but are now just coasting along; and
  3 organizations that are in decline.
- An organization matrix (similar to the Boston Consulting Group matrix) can be developed for organizations plotting them against market share and market growth.
- Entrepreneurial organizations usually operate in conditions of high market growth.
- Entrepreneurial organizations will have a portfolio that also contains more mature products that act as *cash cows*.
- *Apostle*-type customers are very important to entrepreneurial organizations as they carry the message about the organization to those they interact with.

- The role of the leader is very important in entrepreneurial organizations, which are often a club/power culture.
- The attributes of excellent companies described by Peters and Waterman are a useful way of considering the differences between entrepreneurial and non-entrepreneurial organizations.
- Nobody, including the leader, is ever dispensable.
- Blame cultures and organizations where staff are afraid of punishment do not have a suitable atmosphere for entrepreneurship.
- Routine tasks and the staff that carry them out are just as important as the more entrepreneurial ones.

At any moment in history there appear to have been, in entrepreneurial terms, three types of organization, both co-existing and competing:

» entrepreneurial organizations;
» organizations that were once entrepreneurial but are now just coasting along; and
» organizations that are in decline.

The Boston Consulting Group in the United States produced the well-known Boston matrix as part of their work on marketing in the 1960s. They defined the position of a product in an organization's portfolio in terms of market share and market growth. The four possible positions for a product are:

» high share/high growth
» low share/high growth
» high share/low growth
» low share/low growth.

The group gave a title to each of these product positions:

» high share/high growth: STAR
» low share/high growth: PROBLEM CHILD
» high share/low growth: CASH COW
» low share/low growth: DOG.

Stars generate cash and profit as the organization has a high share in a market that is growing, whereas a *problem child* has the potential to become a *star* but is not likely to have paid off its development costs yet due to the low market share. However, as the market is one of growth all will be well if the organization can obtain a higher share of that market.

Cash cows generate much of the operational revenue for organizations. They are not spectacular performers as the market growth is slow or even stagnant but the organization has a large share of the market. As these are usually mature products and services it is unlikely that the organization needs to spend much updating production facilities or paying for major advertising etc. *Dogs* on the other hand are losing market share in a declining market and the organization should divest itself of them as soon as possible. One of the ways that decline can be averted is through segment shift as introduced in Chapter 3. A product that is a *dog* in one market may well be a *star* and eventually a *cash cow* in another. The Morris Oxford (a 1950s/60s British motor car) line was sold to India when sales dropped in the UK and, as the Hindustan Ambassador, has been one of the best-selling Indian automobiles for many years - a classic example of segment shift.

Organizations have a very similar matrix, as shown in Fig. 6.1.

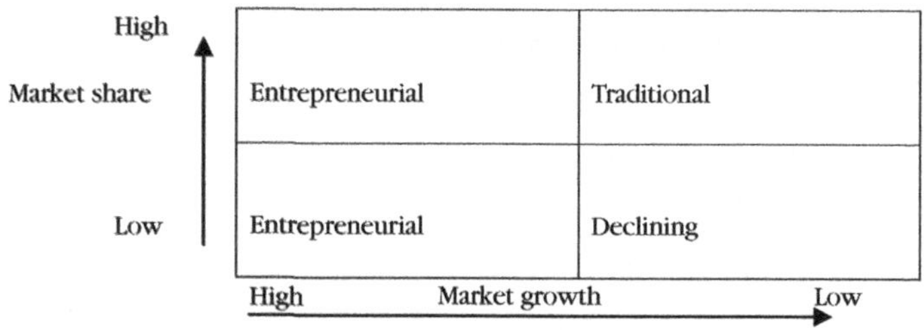

Fig. 6.1 The entrepreneurial matrix.

As can be seen, the entrepreneurial organization operates to the left-hand side of the matrix but this does not mean that such organizations do not have operations centered upon the right-hand side.

THE ENTREPRENEURIAL PORTFOLIO

The contemporary entrepreneurial organization will have a portfolio of products, services, and operations. Whilst many of these will be of an entrepreneurial, cutting edge, growth nature there will be others that are further along the product life cycle and which are more mature and routine. Organizations need to have a balance. *Cash cows* are an important part of the portfolio of any organization as it is they that provide the day-to-day operating revenue for organizations. Without products that bring in a surplus of cash, entrepreneurial products that may have high start-up costs cannot be developed.

It is therefore important that the entrepreneurial organization pays attention to its more routine operations. The organizations mentioned in this material and especially in Chapter 7 - Nokia, P&O, easyJet, Star Cruises, Virgin, and Amazon.com - are highly entrepreneurial but bring the same degree of commitment and customer care to their older products - the products that once were part of their entrepreneurial portfolio and now represent their *cash cows*. It is these products that made their reputations and set standards that newer offerings need to meet.

In the early twenty-first century much of the entrepreneurial activity has been in the ICT and electronics sectors just as in the nineteenth century entrepreneurial activity centered upon transportation, logistics, and domestic products. Being a customer-centered philosophy entrepreneurism is driven by the market. It is not a function of inventors.

In the 1920s and 1930s many entrepreneurial organizations looked at the aircraft industry following the technical innovations of World War I. Eddy, Potter, and Page, writing in 1976, profiled James Smith McDonnell (of McDonnell Aircraft, later McDonnell Douglas, and entrepreneur of St Louis) who believed like many that people are the carvers of their own destiny. Across the United States and Europe entrepreneurs were involved in the building of the fist generation of passenger aircraft that were safe and reliable, such as the Douglas DC3 (the Dakota of World War II fame), or founding the first international airlines such as TWA, Pan Am, Lufthansa and Imperial Airways. Having seen technological advances it was the entrepreneurs who turned them into commercial reality. In a similar manner it is entrepreneurs such as Gates at Microsoft and Bezos at Amazon.com who have used ICT developments in a commercial manner and brought the benefits of such developments to a global marketplace.

Many of the most creative minds are not necessarily commercially oriented. Where there is great potential for success there is a partnership of synergy between the creative inventor, a visionary entrepreneur, and somebody who can handle the routines needed for commercial success, a point that will be explored later in this chapter.

Contemporary entrepreneurial organizations are characterized by one overwhelming feature - they know, understand, and care about their customers. They also use their customers to promote the product. Jones and Strasser, writing in the *Harvard Business Review* in 1995, talked about an extremely loyal type of customer they termed an *apostle*. Entrepreneurial organizations cultivate such customers who not only buy from the organization but also actively promote it by singing its praises. The downside is that if such customers cease to be delighted and are let down they can become *terrorists* who switch from praising the company to friends, relatives, and colleagues to damming it with even greater voracity.

THE ROLE OF THE LEADER

Peter Drucker, one of the leading US and world writers on business, makes the point that existing organizations, whether they operate in the private sector for profit or are non-profit public sector operations, often need to change their management style if they intend to adopt an entrepreneurial philosophy.

As values and philosophy often begin at the top of organizations such an approach often requires a change in leadership style and this may well lead to changes in organizational culture.

In an organization's outward dealings the importance of customer relations has already been mentioned, as has the careful consideration of risk. Inwardly entrepreneurial organizations need to allow their staff to take calculated risks without fear of undue punishment and that requires particular leadership skills.

In 1982 Tom Peters and Robert Waterman published *In Search of Excellence*, a study of US organizations that they considered were amongst the most successful at the time. Their work has received some criticism since then, as some of the organizations quoted have been less successful in recent years. However, as earlier chapters in this material showed, organizations go through a life cycle and change so it not surprising if there have been fluctuations of fortune amongst the companies studied. What was of considerable use was their description of a set of attributes of successful and excellent organizations. Their studies concluded that there were eight basic attributes of excellent companies backed up by seven basic beliefs. The basic, underlying beliefs of the excellent organizations studied were:

- a belief in being the best;
- a belief in the importance of getting the details right;

» a belief that the people who worked for the organization were at the heart of its success;
» a belief in superior quality and service;
» a belief in encouraging innovation and tolerating failure where there was a genuine effort to move the organization on;
» a belief in the importance of internal communications; and
» a belief in the need for the organization to grow economically.

Supported by these beliefs, the organizations demonstrated the following eight attributes.

Bias for action

The organizations were ones that were innovative and were willing to try things. This attitude is demonstrated by the organizations considered in this material. They are *proactive* rather than *reactive*.

Closeness to the customer

It is only by talking to customers that you can find out what they want.

Tom Peters has become famous for the phrase "Management by Wandering Around" (MBWA) and stresses the importance of talking to customers, not just to sell but to find out about their wants and needs.

Autonomy and entrepreneurship

Excellent organizations encourage people to take responsibility for decisions within corporate guidelines and in accordance with the mission and vision of the organization.

One key characteristic of an excellent organization is that it realizes the contribution of its entire staff. This means celebrating success throughout the organization. Excellent organizations ensure that internal customers know what is happening and share in good external customer comments.

Hands on, value driven

In excellent organizations, the core values and beliefs of the organization are known and understood by all of the staff. It does not matter whether it is a huge multinational like a regional leader or a small organization, perhaps an independent retailer with one outlet - everybody who works for the organization needs to understand its philosophy and communicate that to the customers and their colleagues, especially new hirings within the organization.

Stick to the knitting

One thing that Peters and Waterman found was that although there may be gaps in unrelated markets, organizations were most successful when they stuck to what they were good at. This does not mean that there should not be diversification, but it does need to be planned and the market analyzed with very great care.

Single form, lean staff

Organizations work best with simple structures. A complex organization often pushes customers from department to department and the more complex an organization is, the more difficulties are encountered with communications.

Productivity through people

One key characteristic of an excellent organization is that it realizes the contribution of its entire staff. This means celebrating success throughout the organization. It ensures that internal customers know what is happening and share in good external customer comments. All quality ultimately depends on the people in the organization.

Simultaneous loose-tight properties

This is a long title for a simple but very important concept. Staff at the customer interface should have as much flexibility and decision-making power as possible but the organization must keep a close control on its core values and finances. Entrepreneurial managers free up people to do what they are good at, having ensured that they understand the values, culture, and the philosophy of the organization.

These values and attributes need to stem from the leader in the organization. Whilst textbooks record a number of different types of leader ranging from traditional dynastic leaders through to those situational leaders who can take command in a crisis, entrepreneurship seems to require a considerable degree of charismatic leadership. This is not surprising as charisma is linked to a sense of vision and mission, and these too are important for entrepreneurship.

Entrepreneurial organizations seem to need a central figure to act as a source of organizational power - a type of culture Charles Handy refers to as a power/club culture in his classic work on organizational cultures, *The Gods of Management* (1978). Such a culture is not without its problems. Unlike a traditional bureaucracy it is not as rule bound, but there are likely to be many informal rules and norms many perhaps instituted by the leader. Handy represents this form of culture by a spider's web and the closer an individual is towards the center where the power lies, the more influence that individual is likely to possess. In many cases the leader may be so strong that once he or she goes (for whatever reason), the organization may begin to come apart. In their 1981 study, *The Art of Japanese Management*, Richard Pascale and Anthony Athos contrasted the US ITT (International Telephone and Telegraph) and the Japanese Matsushita Electric Company. For nearly 20 years before his retirement in 1979 a very dynamic CEO, Harold S. Geneen, managed ITT. As described in their work, Geneen was often referred to as a genius, ambitious, tough, powerful, demanding, and successful. ITT was a highly entrepreneurial company. However, by the late 1970s, Geneen *was* ITT and as the writers report the company began to decline rapidly once he had retired. One of the problems with charismatic leaders is that they often fail to address succession planning.

Leaders in entrepreneurial organizations are often very strong characters indeed and the organization may become totally identified with them. Whilst in the short to medium term this is often beneficial, as with the excellent publicity that Sir Richard Branson's ballooning exploits have provided for the Virgin organization, the question of the long term needs to be addressed. It has often been the case that personalities have become linked almost irrevocably to their organization's name. Examples are J. P. Morgan and the International Mercantile Marine, Cornelius Vanderbilt of the New York Central Railroad, Woolworth and his retail empire, Anita Roddick and Body Shop, Bezos and Amazon.com, and Branson and the Virgin Group.

If the leader is also the owner or majority stock/shareholder this may present problems. If he or she is not then the board need to address the issue decisively but sensitively. It needs to be borne in mind that with the exception of a small number of organizations set up for specific projects, organizations should carry on after staff have retired etc. Nobody, however charismatic they are, should be indispensable.

Work on leadership up to the middle of the twentieth century tended to stress the role of the leader as a controller whilst later writers including Peters and Waterman (introduced earlier in this chapter) in the United States and John Adair in the UK have seen leadership much more in terms of motivating and facilitating. As staff become better educated, a process that went on throughout the twentieth century, leaders need to perform less and less "police"-type roles and more coaching and encouraging. In the entrepreneurial organization this is of especial importance as all staff need to be on message and understand the vision of the organization. This can only be done by encouragement; it cannot be accomplished using orders.

Stephen Covey, an American who has examined the behavior of highly effective individuals in *The 7 Habits of Highly Effective People* (1994) - a book recommended for all who are studying both entrepreneurship and personal development - also looked at leadership in his 1990 text, *Principle Centered Leadership*. In this work Covey made the point that managers and leaders can still remain in overall charge but can and should empower staff. Leaders can be in charge of direction and mission and yet still give those staff who have proved themselves the opportunity to manage their own functions without overt control. In this way staff may be happier to make use of entrepreneurial opportunities.

BLAME AND RISK

At the very beginning of this material it was stated that entrepreneurial organizations were more likely to take a calculated risk than non-entrepreneurial ones. This does not mean that they are foolhardy but that after a careful analysis of the internal and external factors involved, those organizations that are more entrepreneurial are more likely to go for project or product provided that the result of failure does not endanger the survival of the organization.

It might be thought that starting an international airline in the highly competitive market of the mid 1980s when few of the world's airlines were profitable was a risky undertaking. Add to that the fact that the main competitor would be one of the few profitable airlines at the time - British Airways (BA) - and this makes the venture seem even more of a gamble especially when the organization (and its leader) concerned had no experience in the industry. However, Richard (later Sir Richard) Branson and Virgin initially charted a single Boeing 747 for one year and as he states in his autobiography, *Losing my Virginity* (1998), the most the organization would lose would be £2 million per year - a small amount to Virgin. Despite the competition from BA (some of which has been deemed unfair and has been described by Martyn Gregory in his book *Dirty Tricks - British Airways' secret war against Virgin Atlantic* (1994)), Virgin as an air carrier has been very successful and has expanded its route network into Asia and southern Africa. Each development has been a risk but a carefully calculated and affordable one.

Blame

The managing director of a UK company once remarked in the author's presence that he would rather staff came to him for forgiveness than for permission. As he had ensured that all staff understood the philosophy of the organization and the limits of their authority this was not too dangerous a statement. What he wanted was staff who would take responsibility for solving problems. That is difficult to do in a punishment-centered blame culture.

One of the problems that has beset both US and European organizations recently is the issue of short-termism. Many institutional share/stockholders require an ROI (return on investment) of about 15% per annum. By contrast many Asian organizations have preferred a lower ROI but to build up market share. Whilst an ROI of 15% may not be unreasonable for a mature company, entrepreneurial organizations may require a considerable amount of time building up a customer/product base before such an ROI becomes a possibility. However, if managers are to be punished for not achieving such results they are likely to adopt short term, low risk approaches which may do nothing to grow the company's customer base and reputation but only generate immediate profits which may not be sustainable.

It is almost impossible for an organization to be entrepreneurial if its members are watching their backs all the time. People have to be allowed to make genuine mistakes provided that they learn from them. It is often said that far more is learnt from things that go wrong than things that go right!

This does not mean that those who do not learn or those that exceed their authority should not be censored - they should. However, honest mistakes that aid organizational learning and development can be tolerated as they may be the foundation of future progress.

ENTREPRENEURIAL AND ROUTINE STAFF

However entrepreneurial an organization is and however much vision fills the leadership it still has to compete in a harsh competitive world. Whilst the entrepreneurial aspects of the organization may be the glamorous part, routine tasks need to be carried out with just as much focus on quality.

Entrepreneurial organizations need staff to carry out the routine tasks that are required for any business to function properly. Not everybody has an entrepreneurial mindset and those who do not may find the way the more entrepreneurial staff operate disquieting and even chaotic. It is incumbent on those in managerial and leadership positions to make sure that such staff understand what is happening in the organization and why. Entrepreneurially oriented staff may find that routine tasks required of them are tedious or boring and they may fail to pass on information to staff dealing with routine matters. They need to be made aware of why such information is important. As has already been stressed in this material, the modern entrepreneurial organization is a balance between those working at the entrepreneurial tasks and those supporting them through routine operations. Both are just as important to the effectiveness and efficiency of the organization.

The UK researcher Meredith Belbin has studied the composition of effective and ineffective teams and has concluded that teams need a balance of team role personalities within them. They need members who are creative, challenging, and entrepreneurial, but also those who are suited to the discipline and focus of routines. An entrepreneurial organization can learn much from studies in effective teamwork, especially the need for this balance. Whilst an organization of routine-minded people might never have an entrepreneurial idea, an organization full of entrepreneurs might have problems ordering and paying for supplies etc. - routine tasks that require a different approach.

The future

Just as entrepreneurial organizations have always been with us, there will always be those at the cutting edge of growth in the future. Whatever the area of operations it is safe to say that the entrepreneurial organizations of the future will:

» research their markets;
» take calculated risks;
» understand their customers;
» have vision;
» believe in themselves;
» be at the cutting edge of developments; and
» adapt to change.

Others may follow but for those who can stand the pace, the entrepreneurial organization is likely to be where the action is hottest and each day is probably different.

KEY LEARNING POINTS

» Even entrepreneurial organizations require a balance between those involved on entrepreneurial activities and those carrying out routine tasks.
» If an organization wishes to be entrepreneurial it needs to ensure that staff understand the organizational philosophy and culture and the limits of their responsibility.
» Staff who ask for forgiveness rather than permission are more likely to move the organization forward.
» Short term financial gain is no substitute for longer term market penetration.
» The role of the leader is crucial to entrepreneurial organizations, as is the need to ensure a policy of succession.

The Entrepreneurial Organization – Success Stories

» Microsoft - US and global
» easyJet - Europe
» Star Cruises - Asia

MICROSOFT - US AND GLOBAL

Amongst the names that have become synonymous with the development and use of ICT are Microsoft and its founders Bill Gates (the richest man in the United States) and Paul Allen.

The success of Microsoft and its domination of the personal computer software market through the Windows operating system stems from the entrepreneurial nature of the company's founders, William Henry (Bill) Gates and Paul Allen. This section is concerned with Microsoft as an organization and whilst that success cannot be decoupled from the personal and technical characteristics of Gates specifically, the section will concentrate on organizational issues. There is more material on Gates the individual in *The Entrepreneurial Individual*, another title in the ExpressExec series.

Gates formed his first company whilst still in high school. He had shown an aptitude for computer technology and devised a system for carrying out traffic counts. The 1970 saw the beginnings of a hobby market in self-build primitive computers. The introduction of kits for the Altair 880 system in 1975 provided Gates and Allen with the opportunity to write software to use on the machine. Interestingly software was the neglected area of development. At that time the "intellectual" stimulation of building a machine that would work seemed to be the main focus of hobbyists.

It was very astute and highly entrepreneurial of Gates and Allen to realize that their futures lay not in designing and supplying hardware but in providing the software for such machines.

Gates's great contribution may well be remembered not so much in the names of his products but in his realization that the developing IT (information technology) sector would eventually require standardization. In the beginning each machine used its own, sometimes unique, operating system. Gates foresaw that compatibility would be the route to success.

Original equipment manufacturers (OEMs)

Many of the early computer enterprises were concerned with the development of small machines suitable for desktop use, what has become known as the PC (personal computer) - a term originally applied to the products of IBM (International Business Machines), a company that entered the market quite late having previously concentrated on mainframe hardware. Many of the names now belong to history but PET, Sirius, Apricot, etc., were the first generation of office computers and needed applications to run on them. From early on users required word processing and spreadsheets, WordStar and SuperCalc being two of the earliest examples of applications written for different machines but overlaid on the operating system so that the same commands would operate them once the machine was booted. There was also a growing games market, primitive as the early offerings were, as users realized the "fun" and entertainment potential of computers.

Whilst there might have been a temptation to go into hardware manufacture, Gates took the view that the future of Microsoft lay in providing applications etc. for a range of hardware and that Microsoft should enter into partnership agreements with OEMs (original equipment manufacturers). Microsoft would provide DOS (disk operating system) and applications for a manufacturer's machines and whilst each version might be slightly different due to the design of the hardware, the user would not notice this. The concept of a "one size fits all" approach to software is what has made Microsoft the force in the world that it is today. No matter who made the hardware by forming an early partnership with that OEM, by the time the equipment reached the market, Microsoft would have software available.

Packages

It was but a short step from having applications available for a new computer system at its launch to having it already pre-installed, making the whole package ready to run from the box - a considerable boon to the growing number of users who had no interest in computers as technology but who needed the applications for their work and pleasure. They did not want to go through a process of installing software; they wanted the whole package ready to run.

The development of Windows as an operating environment originally by Apple but later becoming a name synonymous with Microsoft allowed for multi-functionality and multi-tasking to be offered to even the most inexperienced user. Packages such as Microsoft Office, containing as they do a word processor (Word) and a spreadsheet

(Excel), etc., provide for a complete set of applications using similar commands and icons, all in a mouse-driven, Windows environment.

Microsoft is not alone in offering such packages: Lotus Development Corporation's Lotus 1-2-3 is a very popular product and is used by many commercial users.

Operating systems

The very earliest machines were devoid of the hard disks and even monitors that are the norm today. In order to start up the hardware it had to be booted (derived from "pulling it up by the bootstraps"), adding an operating system to the small amount of resident instructions.

As an internal hard disk became the norm it was necessary to develop what we now know as DOS software to manage the computer system.

Microsoft's growth is in part because of the development of MS-DOS as this standardized operating system has become the platform upon which Windows can be placed and the myriad of Microsoft and other Windows-compatible applications run.

DOS has had competitors, notably OS/2, but the world appears to have accepted DOS as the standard. The development of computer networks and the importance of communication between machines predicated the adoption of a common standard. Computers are not alone in this respect. Hobbies such as model railroading have been required to adopt common scales, and as electronic control becomes the norm, common control systems and standard setting bodies, e.g. the NMRA (National Model Railroaders of America) standards for equipment. It is a feature of the growth of globalization that individual companies and even countries can no longer afford to be out of step with each other. Compatibility is all-important, a point stressed in the ExpressExec material on *Going Global* that also features in this series.

Microsoft has made compatibility its stock in trade, compatibility that is actually on the terms of Microsoft has been setting the compatibility standards, in effect writing the rules, and nothing is as fundamental in the computer business as the operating system.

BASIC

In 1964 as a result of an NSF (National Science Foundation) grant, John Chimney and Thomas Kurt at Dartmouth College ran the first example of a new programming language called BASIC (Beginners All-purpose Symbolic Instruction Code). The important thing about BASIC was that it began the process of demystifying programming. It was an object lesson in simplicity. On the wall of the study of the writer of this material is a certificate dating from 1985 entitled Certificate in Computer Literacy using BASIC. When the writer wanted the computer to do something it was just a matter of a few simple lines of code:

```
10 New
20 PRINT 5 + 3
```

If RUN was then typed the legend:

8

appeared on the screen. In the 1970s this was wonderful and cutting edge!

One of the problems was that there were many forms of BASIC and they all used slightly different syntax. In essence they were dialects and programmers needed to learn a number of variations.

By developing MS (Microsoft) BASIC, the company was able to develop a single basic type. The provision of MS BASIC + MS-DOS by OEMs (see earlier) allowed the computer manufacturers to offer a hardware/software package to customers that did not require any relearning of commands and operating protocols.

Windows

Apple computers were the first to offer an operating environment that used a mouse and icons to point and click rather than keyboard inputs. Indeed one idea was to remove the keyboard completely as some of the small hand-held organizers and computers have done.

Microsoft developed what is now known as Microsoft Windows and this product has gone through a series of developments, Windows 3.1, 95, 98, Millennium, etc., and has become the major system used world-wide. Indeed it was the complete domination of Windows and the fact that more and more computers were being sold not only with Microsoft applications pre-loaded but also with Internet access through a Microsoft application that caused concerns about a Microsoft global monopoly. The world began to ask if Microsoft was controlling access to the Internet for an increasing percentage of the global population. This was a question that the US government put before the courts with the result that Microsoft was ordered to split itself into two separate organizations to avoid any conflict of interest. At the time of writing this issue is at the appeal stage in the US courts.

It is hardly surprising that so many of the world's computers come pre-loaded with Microsoft products and not in the least sinister. Microsoft took an entrepreneurial decision to work with OEMs and provide applications for different computers. That was clearly a sensible commercial decision. Unfortunately the world has become so dependent on ICT that any monopoly looks dangerous - hence the action by the US government.

Like Coca-Cola, Boeing, and Shell, the word Microsoft is a global term; no matter where one is there will probably be a computer running Windows (see Fig. 7.1). Microsoft has not been beyond criticism. OEMs were very good at finding software bugs as they tested their machines before putting them onto the market. Once Microsoft began to supply retailers who dealt directly with the public such bugs were not so easily tolerated. It must be stressed, however, that Microsoft appears to have worked hard at minimizing the effects of such bugs and have rectified any problems quickly. However, computers still crash because of the software but such occurrences seem to be becoming rarer.

KEY INSIGHTS

» Microsoft was founded and driven by a person with vision - Bill Gates.

» The decision to work with OEMs (original equipment manufacturers) rather than develop hardware allowed Microsoft to penetrate the whole of the microcomputer market.

» Working with OEMs from the beginnings of the development of a particular machine gave Microsoft the advantage of being ready with applications as soon as that machine entered the market.

» Users became used to operating Microsoft applications as they traded up equipment.

» Packaging Microsoft software directly onto machines meant that it was possible for users to operate their new equipment straight from the box.

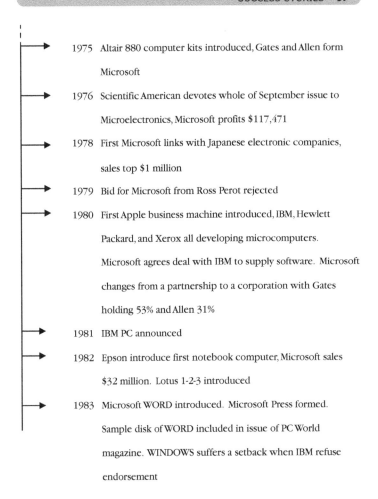

1975 Altair 880 computer kits introduced, Gates and Allen form Microsoft

1976 Scientific American devotes whole of September issue to Microelectronics, Microsoft profits $117,471

1978 First Microsoft links with Japanese electronic companies, sales top $1 million

1979 Bid for Microsoft from Ross Perot rejected

1980 First Apple business machine introduced, IBM, Hewlett Packard, and Xerox all developing microcomputers. Microsoft agrees deal with IBM to supply software. Microsoft changes from a partnership to a corporation with Gates holding 53% and Allen 31%

1981 IBM PC announced

1982 Epson introduce first notebook computer, Microsoft sales $32 million. Lotus 1-2-3 introduced

1983 Microsoft WORD introduced. Microsoft Press formed. Sample disk of WORD included in issue of PC World magazine. WINDOWS suffers a setback when IBM refuse endorsement

Fig. 7.1 Time line for Microsoft's most entrepreneurial activities, 1975–92.

1984 *Fortune* Magazine article about Microsoft dominating the market

1990 WINDOWS 3 introduced

1992 Microsoft and IBM partnership ended

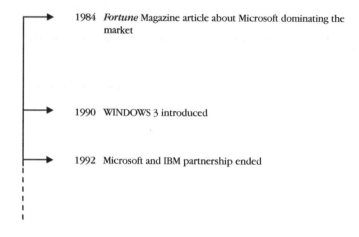

Fig. 7.1 *(continued)*.

» Microsoft has always developed software and applications that are easy for the non-specialist to use.
» The sheer volume of Microsoft products and the cross-use and compatibility between them create a form of dependency amongst users.

EASYJET – EUROPE

Deregulation of airlines under the Republican administrations of the 1980s in the United States led to the growth of a number of low cost airline operations operating within the continental United States. Safety concerns caused some customer resistance and competition from existing operators proved quite intense.

Europe was slower to follow the deregulation path but its introduction from 1987 onwards has led to at least one success story showing how an entrepreneurial organization can break into what had previously been a restricted marketplace.

The low cost, no frills airline easyJet, first introduced in Chapter 4, owes its existence to the development of deregulation and an open skies policy in the Europe Union. Before 1987 European air travel was effectively in the hands of national (and often state-owned) flag-carriers which considered the air routes between the major European cities to be immune from competitive influences, protected as the airlines were by the relevant governments.

Under this system the customer was almost an afterthought as flying schedules, fares, and even the number of passengers that each national airline could carry were negotiated between governments through "bilateral" agreements that had little element of competition. Competition from other airlines was almost unheard of, so regulated was the market, a problem that was analyzed by Sampson in *Empires of the Sky* as early as 1984.

Despite opposition from a number of EU member states wanting to protect their own state-owned airlines from competition, the European Commission introduced its three-phase 10-year reform process in 1987. At the present time any airline holding a valid Air Operators Certificate in the EU cannot be prevented from operating on any route within the EU, including flights wholly within another country. This is one of the "freedoms of the air," in fact the seventh freedom - the right of an airline to pick up passengers in one country and to fly them to another country without stopping in the airline's home country. Such granting of seventh freedom rights to EU airlines is wholly consistent with EU policy on the movement of citizens around the Union.

easyJet commenced flight operations as a low cost airline in November 1995. The airline initially operated just two routes from Luton (outside London) to Glasgow and Edinburgh in Scotland. At that time the company had two Boeing 737 aircraft. By 2001 the airline had grown to 35 routes from 16 European airports and was flying 21 Boeing 737 aircraft. During the financial year to September 30, 2000, the company reported pre-tax profits of £22 million on a turnover of £263 million and carried 5.6 million passengers. The airline went public with a share offering on the London Stock Exchange on November 22, 2000. The airline raised £195.3 million and was valued at £777 million at flotation. Despite being offered only to financial institutions, the shares were oversubscribed by a factor of nearly 10.

easyJet is majority owned by the wealthy Haji-Ioannou family. Stelios Haji-Ioannou, the driving force behind easyJet is a high profile entrepreneur who also controls other separate easyGroup companies such as easyEverything, easyRentacar, and easyValue. Whilst there is no formal cross-shareholdings between easyJet and these other easyGroup companies, some cross-marketing agreements do exist; for example, initial easyRentacar sites were at destinations served by easyJet. The airline is based at Luton Airport to the North of London. The opening of a rail station at Luton Airport with services directly to the center of London has relieved the problem of customers having to take a bus to the main station in Luton and transfer to trains.

How easyJet keeps its prices low but still delivers a quality product

easyJet keeps costs low by eliminating the unnecessary costs and frills, which characterize more conventional airlines. This is done in a number of ways.

- Use of the Internet to reduce distribution costs, as discussed in Chapter 4. easyJet operates under the branding of "the web's favorite airline," based on the fact that it sells a higher proportion of seats online, through easyJet.com, than any other airline. easyJet was one of the first airlines to embrace the opportunity of the Internet when it sold its first seat online in April 1998. In January 2001 approximately 86% of all seats were sold over the Internet, making it one of the UK's biggest Internet retailers.
- Maximize the utilization of the substantial assets. Each new Boeing 737 aircraft has a list price in the region of $35 million. Therefore maximizing utilization of each aircraft reduces the unit cost. Turnaround times are kept to the minimum - an aircraft on the ground and empty of passengers is earning no revenue.
- Direct sell only. easyJet only sells tickets over the Internet, through the telephone sales center or, to a much lesser extent, at an airport sales desk. This means there are no intermediaries adding unnecessary costs.
- Ticketless travel. Passengers instead receive an e-mail containing their travel details and confirmation number when they book online.

This helps to reduce significantly the cost of issuing, distributing, processing, and reconciling millions of tickets each year.

» Elimination of free meals and drinks on-board. Eliminating free catering on-board reduces cost and unnecessary bureaucracy and management. It is also an important differentiator between easyJet and other airlines and a reflection of the easyJet no frills, low cost approach. Passengers can purchase food and drinks on-board.
» Use the most appropriate airports. Within the UK, easyJet uses smaller airports as its base airports. Not only are smaller airports - such as London, Luton, or Liverpool - cheaper to fly from than bigger airports such as Heathrow, Gatwick, or Manchester - but also they are much less congested and turnaround times for aircraft are considerably shorter. By reducing turnarounds to 30 minutes and below, easyJet can achieve extra rotations on the high frequency routes, thereby maximizing utilization rates of its aircraft.
» One kind of aircraft. easyJet only operates the Boeing 737 series aircraft, the best-selling jet aircraft in history. Each aircraft has 149 seats. Commonality maximizes efficiency in the recruitment and training of staff (engineers, pilots, cabin crew, etc.) and allows the airline to move aircraft around the network with greater ease than a traditional airline, which may have many different aircraft types.
» Paperless operations. Since its launch easyJet has simplified its working practices by embracing the concept of the paperless office. The management and administration of the company is undertaken entirely on IT systems which can be accessed through secure servers from anywhere in the world enabling huge flexibility in the running of the airline.
» Despite being a low cost airline easyJet trains its staff well not only in the safety aspects required by law, but also in customer care. Operating in a low cost environment can mean that customers unused to airline procedures travel with the airline and may not be aware of the legal and safety requirements that compel the airline to take some of the actions it does.

In 2000 and 2001 easyJet was the subject of a documentary series broadcast by one of the UK commercial television stations. The programs showed the good and the not so good sides of the operation. Some customers were rude, even abusive. easyJet's low cost approach means that there is not the flexible ticketing that more traditional airlines operate. Customers who have paid only £29 ($47) for a single ticket from Luton to Glasgow should not be surprised if there is a hefty surcharge should they miss their flight. However, as is human nature some are very upset. The author traveled on easyJet in the course of researching this material and on one occasion was delayed from catching a flight by a rail connection *en route* to Luton. It must be said that easyJet could not have been more helpful although an extra payment was (quite rightly) requested.

Like most low cost operators the later a ticket is booked, the more it costs, and thus a late change is treated as a late booking.

easyJet – a European airline

easyJet has four main operating bases - London Luton, Liverpool, Geneva, and Amsterdam. It is a truly European operation and was one of the few airlines to take advantage of the reforms offered by the single European aviation market as discussed above. easyJet, which employs almost 1400 people, currently has 18 Boeing 737-300 aircraft and 3 Boeing Next Generation 737-700s. In March 2000, it placed an order for 17 brand-new Boeing 737-700 aircraft for delivery by the end of 2004. This was in addition to an existing order for 15 of the same kind of aircraft. The first aircraft of this type was delivered in October 2000. By 2004, allowing for some retirements, the airline will have a total of 44 aircraft and price protection rights on a further 30. By this time the average age of the aircraft in the fleet will be less than 4 years, making it one of the youngest in the world.

The culture of easyJet

easyJet operates an informal company culture with a very flat management structure, which eliminates unnecessary and wasteful layers of management. This type of flat structure is typical of entrepreneurial organizations where the source of executive power is often vested in a small number of senior managers or even a single entrepreneurial individual, in this case Stelios Haji-Ioannou. All office-based employees are encouraged to dress casually. Ties are apparently banned - except for pilots! Home working from remote sites and hot-desking (the practice whereby desks are not allocated to individuals but are used as and when required by whoever is working in that area, which necessitates leaving desktops clear) have been characteristics of easyJet since the beginning, again not unusual developments in a young entrepreneurial company.

The low cost European air travel market

The overall air transport market in Europe is expected to grow substantially in the coming years. The International Air Transport Association estimates that the number of international scheduled passengers traveling between countries in Europe will grow from 176 million in 1999 to 215 million in 2003, reflecting an average annual growth rate of 5.1%. By contrast, the low fare segment of the market is expected to grow at a significantly higher rate. It is estimated that low cost airlines which carried 4% of all domestic and international passengers within Europe in 1999 will increase that to a figure 12–15% by 2010 making them major players in the European air travel market.

The low cost market segment is a very diverse one indeed. Within the UK the easyJet operation (and the operations of its major competitors GO and Ryan Air) offers facilities to both leisure and business travelers. Given that the flight times from Glasgow and Edinburgh to Luton are less than an hour the customer has no real need of a food and drinks service as there are excellent facilities at the airport. As mentioned earlier, the building of a rail-air interchange at Luton has greatly aided the business traveler use of both Luton, previously mainly a holiday charter airport, and easyJet. Luton is used as the hub of easyJet's hub and spoke operation with virtually all flights departing or arriving there.

Low cost airlines have brought the possibility of inexpensive breaks abroad to the leisure market and have made business travel considerably less expensive. easyJet does not offer the same frequent flyer programs as traditional airlines, this being one way of keeping its costs down. A number of Scottish organizations have stated to the author that the availability of Scotland-London flights on easyJet has greatly decreased their travel expenditure.

Passenger statistics

As the growing passenger figures detailed in Tables 7.1 and 7.2 indicate, since its advent in 1995 easyJet has made air travel an affordable option for many more people by offering a reliable, quality service at fares that are below the norm for the UK and Europe.

Table 7.1 easyJet passenger numbers (source: easyJet Website).

Year	Passenger total (000)
1995	30
1996	420
1997	1140
1998	1180
1999	3670
2000	5996

Table 7.2 easyJet revenue and profit (source easyJet Website).

Year to end September	Revenue (£m)	Profit (£m)
1998	77.0	5.9
1999	139.8	1.3
2000	263.7	22.1

Financial information

easyJet and its charismatic chairman have clearly chosen the market well. The fare levels are low enough to tempt those who might previously not have considered an airline for their break or business travel. The importance of analyzing the environment has been stressed in this material. The deregulation of European air transportation was the type of political factor that allowed an entrepreneur such as Stelios Haji-Ioannou to take speedy advantage of an opportunity. By offering what his customer base wants - value for money, the routes they require, and safety - he has been able to build up a successful operation in a very short period of time (see Fig. 7.2). That he has charisma, as was shown by his television appearances in the UK documentary - *Airline* - as described earlier, is another factor in making easyJet one of Europe's

- 1987 Deregulation of European air transport
- 1995 First easyJet flights, 2 routes + 2 aircraft, 30,000 passengers
- 1998 First sales online, passengers 1,880,000, profits £5.9 million
- 2000 easyJet floated on London Stock Exchange, passengers 5,996,000, profits £22.1 million
- 2001 35 routes + 21 aircraft
- 2004 (predicted) 44 aircraft

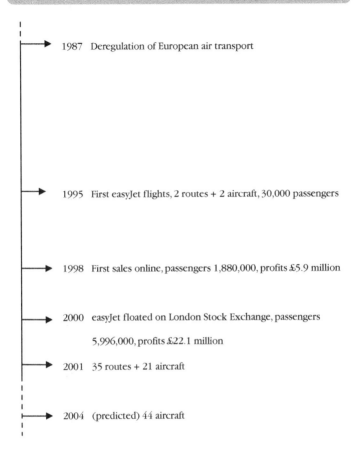

Fig. 7.2 Time line.

leading entrepreneurial organizations. Other airlines have their names emblazoned on their aircraft - easyJet does the same but adds the telephone number and the Web address in large bright-orange numbers and letters as well!

KEY INSIGHTS

The success of easyJet is due not to a single factor but to a combination of opportunities and the commercial acumen of a charismatic leader.

» The decision by the EU to deregulate the airline industry.
» The availability of Boeing 737 aircraft.
» The personal wealth of the Haji-Ioannou family.
» The availability of Luton as an alternative London airport.
» The use of the Internet as both an information and a booking channel.
» The personal charisma of Stelios Haji-Ioannou.

To the above must be added the ability to create a new market for those who had not previously considered air travel due to the high fares, and changing the business market to make business travel more affordable.

The threats to easyJet come from other low cost competitors and the price of fuel. Low fares tend to mean lower margins (although easyJet has quite high load factors on its aircraft due to more customers because of lower fares) and a rise in the global price of oil can erode margins very quickly.

STAR CRUISES – ASIA

Considering that the advent of the jet airliner caused many pundits to write off the large passenger liner as something that the world would never need or see again, it is interesting to note that more and more and larger and larger passenger ships are currently coming into service. However, whilst the *Queen Mary*, the *Normandie* and the *United States* were designed for fast passages between points A and B (New York and Europe in the case of these three) their newer and often larger successors are designed for the cruise industry - floating resorts to provide floating vacations.

As Table 7.3 shows, this is an industry that has almost doubled its customer base in seven years, growth rates that any industry would be happy to achieve.

Table 7.3 Growth in cruise customers, 1992–9.

	1992	1999
US + Canada	4,250,000	6,500,000
UK	225,000	746,000
Asia excluding Japan	75,000	800,000
Japan	20,000	200,000
Other	840,000	1.204,000
Total	*5,410,000*	*9,450,000*

Whilst the US cruise industry grew very rapidly in the 1970s and 1980s it only increased by about 50% in the 1990s, whereas the UK market has tripled and that for both Japan and the rest of Asia has increased by a factor of 10.

There are very good reasons why people have begun to take cruise vacations, including increases in disposable income, marketing of the product to a younger, family market, the safety such a form of travel offers, relaxation, etc.

Prior to the mid 1990s much of the marketing effort and shipbuilding were directed towards the US market but in 1993 a Singapore-based Chinese–Malaysian entrepreneur named Lim Goh Tong brought cruise vacations into the Asian market as a mainstream product.

(Note that, in order to have a common denominator when discussing the size of passenger ships it is customary to use the gross registered tonnage (GRT). GRT is not a measure of weight but of capacity and is the total enclosed volume of the ship in cubic feet divided by 100. The word tonnage comes from the mediaeval "tun" meaning a barrel. This is the normal method of describing the size of a merchant vessel and is measured in accordance with the International Convention on Tonnage Measurement that came into force on July 18, 1982.)

Lim's first business ventures involved the gambling industry - a thriving sector in Asia. Interestingly, casinos are major revenue earners on modern cruise ships especially those operating in both the US and the Asian markets but less so in Europe.

As Cartwright and Baird remarked in their 1999 study of the cruise industry, *The Development and Growth of the Cruise Industry*, it was quite clear that Asia was a potentially huge growth market. The political unrest that had bedeviled Indo-China was in the past thus providing firstly a potential source of customers, but more importantly new destinations. These destinations would be of interest not only to the Asian customer, but also to European vacationers as areas such as Thailand became major long haul tourist destinations. Thus a well-founded Asian cruise company would have two ready markets. Many of the Asian economies were booming in the 1990s and those with wealth needed somewhere to spend it.

Lim's Star Cruises spent $250 million acquiring an initial fleet and another $700 million in orders for new ships. Whilst the original ships were available they had small cabins, but this does not seem to have a problem in the Asian market.

Both Asians and Europeans began to patronize the new company with UK package tour operators such as Thomson Holidays including a Star Cruises package as an optional part of a Thailand land-based vacation.

Lim's coup was to acquire the number 4 player in the market, NCL (Norwegian Cruise Lines), in a $1.9 billion cash and debt deal in 1999, thus outbidding Carnival Cruises' lower offer. Carnival Cruises had already acquired the Orient Line and its ship the *Marco Polo* in 1998. The NCL brand has been kept in the same manner as NCL kept the Orient Line brand name, thus helping to retain the customer base.

Both companies operate at the standard end of the market and are not offering luxury cruises to the very wealthy but value for money vacation packages for a larger number of those with disposable incomes who can afford a holiday at the top of the standard price ranges.

Thus from nothing in the early 1990s, by 2001 the Star Cruises operation comprised the vessels listed in Table 7.4.

Table 7.4 List of Star Cruises vessels..

Name	Size GRT	Acquired	Acquired from	Passengers (maximum)
Star Aquarius	40,012	1993	Converted ferry	1,900
Star Pisces	40,022	1993	Converted ferry	2,000
Superstar Gemini	19,046	1995	Cunard Crown	900
Superstar Capricorn Sold 2000	28,078	1997	Princess Cruises	
Superstar Leo	74,500	1998	New	2,800
Superstar Sagittarius Sold 2000	18,556	1998	Royal Viking	
Superstar Virgo	74,500	1999	New	2,800
Superstar Europe renamed Superstar Aries 1001	37,012	1998/ 2001	From ND Lloyd	1,006
Superstar Libra	91,000	2001	New	4,000
Superstar Taurus	25,000	2000	NCL	1,150
Megastar Aries	3,300	2000	Classical Cruises	80
Megastar Capricorn	4,200	2000	Sun Cruises	135
Megastar Sagittarius	4,200	2000	Sun Cruises	135
Megastar Taurus	3,300	2000	Classical Cruises	80

Building three ships of a total GRT of 315,000.

Ship	GRT	Owner	Maximum passengers
Norway*	76,049	NCL	2,370
Norwegian Dream	50,760	NCL	2,159
Norwegian Majesty	40,876	NCL	1,790
Norwegian Sea	42,267	NCL	1,798
Norwegian Sky	77,104	NCL	2,450
Norwegian Star	28,078	NCL	848 (Australian market)
Norwegian Sun	77,104	NCL	2,450
Norwegian Wind	50,760	NCL	2,156
Building for 2002	80,000	NCL	
Marco Polo	20,502	Orient lines	915

Ex transatlantic line SS France–to be sold 2001/2.

1984 *Fortune* Magazine article about Microsoft dominating the market

1990 WINDOWS 3 introduced

1992 Microsoft and IBM partnership ended

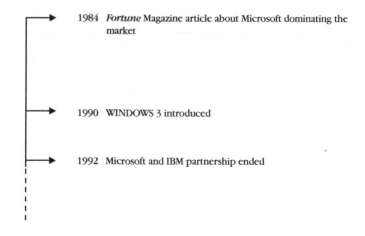

Fig. 7.3 Time line.

These figures give the Star Cruises/NCL operation a total of over 1.7 million GRT by 2004. This will rival the US Carnival Group (Carnival Cruises, Cunard, Costa, Holland America, Seabourne, Windstar plus a stake in the UK Airtours operation), currently holding the number one spot - all in less than 10 years.

The four smaller Star Cruises ships are more akin to private yachts and are available for charter. The NCL ships with one exception have entertainment and catering designed for the US market and operate cruises all over the world.

The Star Cruises ships are predominantly for the Asian market and combine Asian and Western entertainment and catering.

As with other entrepreneurs Lim's ability has been to see a potential market and then use his resources to build a market presence in the shortest possible time (see Fig. 7.3). Had he tried to do this in the Caribbean it is likely that the established companies might have reacted with aggressive competition. Lim's skill was to operate in a market he knew and one that although ripe for expansion had not apparently been targeted by the traditional providers of cruise holidays - one of which he later bought!

KEY INSIGHTS

- Lim Goh Tong entered a market that was ripe with potential but did not appear to be attracting the attention of established operators.
- Vessels were available for purchase leading to a rapid introduction of the product.
- The product has been carefully tailored to the existing and potential customer base.
- Further expansion into established markets has been made through the acquisition of an established operator.
- The brand name of NCL has been kept thus helping to retain its customer base.

02.10.08

Key Concepts and Thinkers in Organizational Entrepreneurship

» Glossary
» Key thinkers.

A GLOSSARY FOR THE ENTREPRENEURIAL ORGANIZATION

Boston matrix - A model for product portfolios developed by the Boston Consulting Group. The model locates products and services in a matrix with the axes of market share and market growth. See Cash cows, Dogs, Problem child, and Star.

Cash cow (Boston matrix) - A product/service for which the organization has a high market share in a low growth market. It is cash cows that provide much of the organization's revenue as production costs etc. are usually quite low and development costs will have been recouped. They are the bread and butter products for organizations.

Culture - The values, attitudes, and beliefs ascribed to and accepted by a group, nation, or organization. In effect, "the way we do things around here."

Dogs (Boston matrix) - Those products/services for which the organization has a low market share in a low growth or even a declining market. They are a drain on resources. Even if they cost little to produce they still tie up staff time and production facilities.

Entrepreneurial organization - An organization concerned with growth and proactivity rather than survival and stability.

Entrepreneurial portfolio - A similar model to the Boston matrix but which looks at products and services from an entrepreneurial point of view. Entrepreneurial products/services tend to be characterized by high market growth.

Organization - The structure set up as a human strategy for achieving a desired goal.

Organizational life cycle - The stages that an organization passes through. Like the human life cycle each stage is characterized by different behavior patterns.

Problem child (Boston matrix) - A product/service for which the organization has a low market share but in a market that is growing. A problem child may well carry considerable development and introduction costs that will need to be recouped. If the organization can gain more market share the problem child may become a star.

Routines - Tasks that need to be undertaken regularly and which are concerned with the maintenance of organizational operations or customer relationships.

Segment shift - The movement of a product or service (or indeed the whole organization) into a different segment of the market.

Short-termism - The application of performance criteria such as ROI (return on investment) that only measure the immediate performance of an organization and not the long term potential. Western organizations and investors often use an ROI of about 15% as an indicator of acceptable performance. Entrepreneurial organizations may be more interested in the growth of market share as this is an indicator of longer term performance. High ROIs are hard to achieve quickly for new products as time is need for the market to be penetrated.

SPECTACLES analysis - An analysis that considers the Social, Political, Economic, Cultural, Technological, Aesthetic, Customer, Legal, Environmental and Sectoral external factors that provide opportunities and threats to the organization. Entrepreneurial organizations monitor these factors regularly in order to be in a position to grasp an opportunity as soon as possible.

Star (Boston matrix) - A product/service with high market share in a high growth market, i.e. the best of both worlds.

SWOT analysis - An analysis that combines the external opportunities and threats from the SPECTACLES analysis with a consideration of the strengths and weaknesses of the organization.

Synergy - A phenomenon where the sum of the parts is greater than the whole. A team of five working in synergy will produce the output of six.

Team role - A person's tendency to behave in a certain way when working in a team situation (see also Team role theory).

Team role theory - a concept pioneered by Meredith Belbin in the UK proposing that a successful team contains individuals who take up specific team roles based on personality in addition to their functional work roles (see also Team role).

KEY THINKERS

All of the books referred to in this section are listed fully in Chapter 9.

Adair, John

Appointed as the world's first Professor of Leadership Studies at Surrey University in 1978, John Adair is currently Visiting Professor of Leadership Studies at the University of Exeter in the south-west of England. Professor Adair has been named as one of 40 people world-wide who have contributed most to the development of management thought and practices - a considerable accolade indeed. Much of his early thinking was influenced by his army career.

He has also operated as a consultant for a wide range of UK and international companies, including Shell, Honeywell, Mercedes and Unilever. Working with ICI (Imperial Chemical Industries) for nearly 10 years, he assisted the company to develop the "manager - leader" concept, which supported ICI in becoming the first British company to make £1 billion pounds profit in 1986 and has formed the basis for much of the development of the leadership concepts that appear in his books.

The key Adair message is that no organization or enterprise can function adequately without good leadership. Although management techniques such as team building and empowerment have changed the manager's role, leadership is still vital for both the attainment of long term goals and maintaining a sense of purpose throughout day-to-day activities. A key leadership function of managers is to lead their staff and make the move from planning to action. Adair has stressed the need for good leaders and managers to take note of the needs of the task but also the needs of the group and the individual needs of staff, striking a dynamic balance amongst the three.

Adair is the author of 26 books and numerous articles on leadership and management development, read by a large number of managers throughout the world, and used by many students undertaking management development courses and programs. His span of managerial subjects is wide ranging, from leadership (for which he is best known) through to decision making. The whole range is of interest to the entrepreneurial organization as it covers areas that will assist in giving the organization a competitive advantage.

Highlights

Books:

» *Not Bosses but Leaders* (1988)

- *Great Leaders* (1989)
- *Understanding Motivation* (1990)
- *Effective Communication* (1997)
- *The John Adair Handbook of Management and Leadership (1998)*
- *John Adair's 100 Greatest Ideas for Effective Leadership and Management* (2001)

Belbin, Meredith

Working from the 1980s onwards Meredith Belbin proposed the concept of team roles and used it to study successful and unsuccessful teams. As covered earlier, teamwork is of vital importance to the entrepreneurial organization. His work was first used in the UK but has since spread throughout the world and is used in team building and as a recruitment aid by many organizations. The nine team roles that Belbin proposed need to be present in a team to ensure the necessary balance and synergy for effective performance. Thus diversity in team membership is to be welcomed and it is important that organizations achieve a diversity and balance between those in entrepreneurial roles and those whose work is more routine. Individuals can be tested for their preferred roles using a questionnaire and Belbin Associates' INTERPLACE® software. Belbin's later work has linked team role theory to organizational design.

There is more information on Belbin's work in *Managing Diversity*, another title in the ExpressExec series.

Highlights

Books:

- *Management Teams-Why they Succeed or Fail* (1981)
- *Team Roles at Work* (1993)
- *The Coming Shape of Organization* (1996)

Other:

- INTERPLACE® software for team role profiling

Drucker, Peter

Born in Vienna in 1909 Peter Drucker has been a major force in managerial and organization thinking since publishing his first ideas in 1939.

Drucker has shown a lifelong appreciation of the creative possibilities of business. His ideas helped shape the dramatic expansion of American industry in the period after World War II and influenced world-wide thinking about business.

Drucker believes that although it is not so very difficult to predict the future, it is only pointless. Many futurologists make quite accurate predictions. They do a good job of foretelling some, but not always the most important, things. To Drucker far more important are the fundamental changes that happened though no one predicted them or could possibly have predicted them. He believes that organizations and individuals cannot make decision for the future. Decisions are commitments to action and actions are always in the present. However, actions in the present are also the one and only way to make the future. Managers are paid to take effective action. That they can do only in contemplation of the present, and by exploiting the changes that have already happened. To enable today's manager to be ahead of this different tomorrow; indeed to make it their tomorrow, is the aim of Drucker in *Managing in Times of Great Change* (1995).

Drucker may not always be the easiest to read but he is one of the most challenging and the entrepreneurial organization will thrive on the challenges that he presents given his vast experience stretching back over many years.

Drucker's autobiography, *Adventures of a Bystander* (he has been anything but!), reflects on his life and those he has met.

In 1985 Drucker turned his attention to entrepreneurship in his book *Innovation and Entrepreneurship* in which he argues for the imposition of discipline in entrepreneurship and innovation in a similar manner to the structured way the Japanese rebuilt their commercial operations post 1945.

There is also the Drucker School of Management and the Peter F. Drucker Foundation for Non-profit Management, both in the United States, the latter concentrating on management functions within public sector (national and local government, military, etc.) operations.

Drucker has produced over 29 separate books and a myriad of articles etc. The most useful from the standpoint of the entrepreneurial organization are listed below:

Highlights

Books:

- *The Practice of Management* (1955)
- *Managing for Results* (1964)
- *Innovation and Entrepreneurship* (1985)
- *Managing for Turbulent Times* (1993)
- *The Executive in Action - Managing for results, innovation and entrepreneurship* (1996)
- *Adventures of a Bystander* (1998)
- *Management Challenges for the 21st Century* (1999)

Farrell, Larry

Farrell has written to explain how the power of entrepreneurship can be harnessed by individuals, organizations, and entire countries to compete and thrive in the twenty-first century. He sees that century as the entrepreneurial age and believes that the twentieth was the managerial age. Examining four fundamental practices of the world's great entrepreneurs, he attempts (successfully) to provide simple strategies for creating and implementing business plans on all levels, from the mission statement to day-to-day organizational practices. Farrell not only offers advice to individual entrepreneurs, but also explains how entrepreneurial culture can be developed and fostered in corporate and governmental settings - hence his importance to this material. In organizational terms he shows how decision makers can facilitate high speed innovation, set free the potential and often hidden genius of the average worker, translate job satisfaction into high quality production, and cultivate customer satisfaction and loyalty.

Immensely readable, Farrell makes the point that anybody or any organization can be entrepreneurial, as it is not so much a "thing" as a way of thinking.

Highlights

Books:

» *The Entrepreneurial Age* (2001)

Heineke, William

Working with journalist Jonathon Marsh, William E. Heineke, the CEO of The Minor Group in Thailand, has produced a guide of 21 Golden Rules for the entrepreneurial global business manager.

Whilst one can sometimes be suspicious of books that seem to offer a shortcut to success, by allying his considerable successful entrepreneurial ability to the skills of his journalist colleague, Heinecke has produced a very useful framework for the entrepreneurial organization to use as it grows and develops.

His 21 Golden Rules may sound a little trite when viewed in isolation but together they provide a powerful and robust structure for an organization to use. They are as follows.

1. Find a vacuum and fill it. (It is worth remembering that a vacuum can be huge or a small niche - fill it and there is no room for anybody else!)
2. Do your homework.
3. You won't be committed if you're not having fun. (The fun side of work is often forgotten and even derided but it can be a crucial motivator.)
4. Work hard, play hard.
5. Work with other people's brains.
6. Set goals (but go easy on vision); note - goals should always be C-SMART (Customer-centered, specific, measurable, agreed, realistic and timely (Cartwright, 2000-*Mastering Customer Relations*).
7. Trust your intuition.
8. Reach for the sky (at least once).
9. Learn to sell.
10. Become a leader.
11. Recognize a failure and move on.
12. Make the most of lucky breaks.

13. Embrace change as a way of life.
14. Develop your contacts.
15. Use your time wisely.
16. Measure for measure (use benchmarking and understand your performance and quality standards).
17. Don't put up with mediocrity.
18. Chase quality not cash.
19. Act quickly in a crisis.
20. After a fall, get back in the saddle quickly.
21. Be content.

Heinecke's work can be reviewed in greater detail in *The Entrepreneurial Individual*, a companion title in the ExpressExec series.

Peters, Tom

From the publication of *In Search of Excellence* in 1982 onwards, Tom Peters has become one of the best known names in the fields of management, change, and quality. His message has been delivered on a global basis and has reached a huge audience, initially of senior but more recently including junior staff.

Three quotes express the importance Tom Peters has had on modern organizational thinking:

> "In no small part, what American corporations have become is what Peters has encouraged them to be."
>
> *The New Yorker*
>
> "Peters is . . . the father of the post-modern corporation."
>
> *Los Angeles Times*
>
> "We live in a Tom Peters world."
>
> *Fortune Magazine*

Tom Peters describes himself as a prince of disorder, champion of bold failures, maestro of zest, professional loudmouth, corporate cheerleader, and a lover of markets. *Fortune Magazine* has also referred to him as the Ur-guru (guru of gurus) of management and compares him to Ralph Waldo Emerson, Henry David Thoreau, and Walt Whitman.

The Economist has titled him as the Uber-guru (literally over-guru). His unconventional views led *Business Week* to describe him as business's best friend and worst nightmare: best friend because of the challenges he throws out which if taken up can lead to success; and worst nightmare because his ideas have challenged conventional thinking – always an uncomfortable thing to do.

Tom followed up on the success of *In Search of Excellence* (1982, with Robert Waterman) with four more best-selling hardback books: *A Passion for Excellence* (1985, with Nancy Austin), *Thriving on Chaos* (1987), *Liberation Management* (1992; acclaimed as the "Management Book of the Decade" for the 1990s), *The Circle of Innovation: You Can't Shrink Your Way to Greatness* (1997), and a pair of best-selling paperback originals, *The Tom Peters Seminar: Crazy Times Call for Crazy Organizations* (1993) and *The Pursuit of WOW!: Every Person's Guide to Topsy-Turvy Times* (1994). The first of Tom's series of books on reinventing work were released in September 1999: *The Brand You50*, *The Project50* (as an e-book, it knocked Stephen King off the top of the e-best-sellers' list!) and *The Professional Service Firm50*. Tom Peters also presents about 100 major seminars globally each year. Organizations pay considerable sums for their staff to attend these seminars. He has also authored hundreds of articles for various newspapers and popular and academic journals, including *Business Week*, *The Economist*, *the Financial Times*, *The Wall Street Journal*, *The New York Times*, *Fast Company*, *The Washington Monthly*, *California Management Review*, *The Academy of Management Review*, *Forbes*, and *The Harvard Business Review*.

Tom Peters's philosophy for the reinvention of business and organizations is about change, giving power to people, and encouraging entrepreneurship. He recognizes that we are in a changing, sometimes chaotic world and sees that as an opportunity, not a threat, for organizations with the courage to move forward. The research for *In Search of Excellence* was under the auspices of the McKinley Organization and was a review of excellent companies in the United States and how it could re-establish its position in world trade. From those early ideas and the attributes contained within (see Chapter 6 of this material) has developed the Peters's philosophy, a philosophy very much concerned with entrepreneurship.

Highlights

Books:

- » *In Search of Excellence* (1982), with Waterman R.
- » *A Passion For Excellence* (1985), with Austin N.
- » *Thriving on Chaos* (1989)
- » *Liberation Management* (1992)
- » *The Pursuit of WOW!* (1994)
- » *The Circle of Innovation* (1997)
- » *The Brand You50* (1999)
- » *The Project50* (1999)
- » *The Professional Service Firm50* (1999)

Other authorities

A number of texts have been produced by and/or about some of the more prominent entrepreneurs and the organizations they have been involved with. Full references for a number of these are provided in Chapter 9.

Many of these texts focus on the personality of the individual entrepreneur but they also include useful organizational insights and background

A small selection of useful tests to read include:

About Amazon.com

- » *Business the Amazon Way*, Saunders R.
- » *Amazon.com*, Spector R.

About Bodyshop

- » *Business as Usual*, Roddick A.
- » *Anita Roddick and the Bodyshop* , Brown P.

About Microsoft

- » *Business the Bill Gates Way*, Dearlove D.
- » *Gates*, Manes S & Andrews P.

About Nokia

- » *Business the Nokia Way*, Merriden T.

About Sony

» ***Made in Japan***, Morita A.

About Virgin

» ***Business the Richard Branson Way***, Dearlove D.
» ***Losing my Virginity***, Branson R.

Resources for the Entrepreneurial Organization

» Books
» Magazines and journals
» Websites.

BOOKS

Note that dates of books in this chapter may differ from those shown in previous chapters. The dates here are of editions that have been revised from the date of first publication as shown in the chapter material.

Adair, J. (1989) *The Action Centred Leader*, The Industrial Society, London.

Adair, J. (1990) *Not Bosses but Leaders*, Kogan Page, London.

Adair, J. (1990) *Understanding Motivation*, Kogan Page, London.

Adair, J. (1997) *Effective Communication*, Pan, London.

Adair, J. (1998) *The John Adair Handbook of Management and Leadership*, Hawkesmere, London.

Adair, J. (2001) *John Adair's 100 Greatest Ideas for Effective Leadership and Management*, Capstone, Oxford.

Belbin, M.R. (1981) *Management Teams - Why they Succeed or Fail*, Heinemann, Oxford.

Belbin, M.R. (1993) *Team Roles at Work*, Butterworth-Heinemann, Oxford.

Belbin, M.R. (1996) *The Coming Shape of Organization*, Butterworth-Heinemann, Oxford.

Branson, R. (1998) *Losing my Virginity*, Virgin Publishing, London.

Brown, P. (1996) *Anita Roddick and the Body Shop*, Exley, London.

Cartwright, R. (2000) *Mastering Customer Relations*, Macmillan, Basingstoke.

Cartwright, R. (2001) *Mastering the Business Environment*, Palgrave (Macmillan), Basingstoke.

Cartwright, R. & Green, G. (1997) *In Charge of Customer Satisfaction*, Blackwell Business, Oxford.

Covey, S.R. (1994) *The 7 Habits of Highly Effective People*, Simon & Schuster, New York.

Covey, S.R. (1990) *Principle-Centered Leadership*, Simon & Schuster, New York.

Dearlove, D. (2001) *Business the Richard Branson Way*, Capstone, Oxford.

Drucker, P. (1955) *The Practice of Management*, Heinemann, Oxford.

Drucker, P. (1985) *Innovation and Entrepreneurship*, Butterworth-Heinemann, Oxford.

Drucker, P. (1993) *Managing for Turbulent Times*, Butterworth-Heinemann, Oxford.

Drucker, P. (1995) *Managing in a Time of Great Change*, Butterworth-Heinemann, Oxford.

Drucker, P. (1996) *The Executive in Action - Managing for results, innovation and entrepreneurship*, HarperCollins, New York.

Drucker, P. (1999) *Adventures of a Bystander*, John Wiley & Sons, London.

Drucker, P. (1999) *Management Challenges for the 21st Century*, Butterworth-Heinemann, Oxford.

Drucker, P. (1999) *Managing for Results*, Heinemann, Oxford.

Eddy, P., Potter, E. & Page, B. (1976) *Destination Disaster*, Hart-Davis, London.

Farrell, L.C. (2001) *The Entrepreneurial Age*, Windsor, Oxford.

Foot, D.K. & Stoffman, D. (1996) *Boom, Bust and Echo*, Macfarlane, Walter & Ross, Toronto, Canada.

Gregory, M. (1994) *Dirty Tricks - British Airways' secret war against Virgin Atlantic*, Little, Brown, London.

Handy, C. (1978) *The Gods of Management*, Souvenir Press, London.

Harris, P.R. & Moran, R.T. (2000) *Managing Cultural Differences*, Gulf Publishing, Houston, TX.

Heinecke, W.E. & Marsh, J. (2000) *The Entrepreneur-21 Golden Rules for the Global Business Manager*, John Wiley & Sons (Asia), Singapore.

Jones, T.O. & Strasser, W.E. Jr (1995) Why Satisfied Customers Defect, *Harvard Business Review*, November-December, pp. 88-99.

Lewis, R.D. (2000) *When Cultures Collide*, Nicholas Brealey, London.

Marquardt, M.J. & Berger, N.O. (2000) *Global Leaders for the 21st Century*, State University of New York Press, Albany, NY.

Morita, A. (1986) *Made in Japan*, HarperCollins, New York.

Pascale, R. & Athos A. (1981) *The Art of Japanese Management*, Simon & Schuster, New York.

Peters, T. (1989) *Thriving on Chaos*, HarperCollins, New York.

Peters, T. (1992) *Liberation Management*, Alfred A Knopf, New York.

Peters, T. (1995) *The Pursuit of WOW!*, Random House, New York.

Peters, T. (1997) *The Circle of Innovation*, Hodder & Stoughton, New York.

Peters, T. (1999) *The Brand You50*, Alfred A Knopf, New York.

Peters, T. (1999) *The Professional Service Firm50*, Alfred A Knopf, New York.

Peters, T. (1999) *The Project50*, Alfred A Knopf, New York.

Peters, T. & Austin, N. (1994) *A Passion for Excellence*, HarperCollins, New York.

Peters, T. & Waterman, R. (1982) *In Search of Excellence*, Harper & Row, New York.

Roddick, A. (2000) *Business as Usual*, HarperCollins, London.

Sampson, A. (1984) *Empires of the Sky*, Hodder & Stoughton, London.

Saunders, R. (2000) *Business the Amazon.com Way*, Capstone, Oxford.

Trompenaars, F. (1993) *Riding the Waves of Culture*, Economist Books, London.

For information about the airline industry in general and comments on easyJet

Hanlon, P. (1999) *Global Airlines*, 2nd edition, Butterworth-Heinemann, Oxford.

For information on the cruise industry

Cartwright, R. & Baird, C. (1999) *The Development and Growth of the Cruise Industry*, Butterworth-Heinemann, Oxford.

Dickinson, R. & Vladimir, A. (1997) *Selling the Sea*, John Wiley & Sons, New York.

For information about Microsoft and Bill Gates

Dearlove, D. (2001) *Doing Business the Bill Gates Way*, Capstone, Oxford.

Manes, S. & Andrews, P. (1994) *Gates*, Simon & Schuster, New York.

For information on Nokia

Merriden, T. (2000) *Cold Calling - Business the Nokia Way*, Capstone, Oxford.

MAGAZINES AND JOURNALS

All broadsheet-type newspapers, *Washington Post*, *New York Times*, *Herald Tribune*, *The Times*, *Daily Telegraph*, *Observer*, *Le Monde*, etc., provide useful analyses of news and financial/business matters. The more those in entrepreneurial organizations know, the further the organization can develop.

The following, most of which are published online as well as in hard copy (see Websites at the end of this chapter), are useful sources of information about markets, competitors, and developments. The Websites should be accessed for subscription rates, samples, and special subscription offers.

Business 2.0

Business and financial daily carrying articles etc. of use to individual entrepreneurs and entrepreneurial organizations.

Financial Times

UK daily carrying financial reports and analyses. Available on subscription or from newsstands.

Forbes

Forbes is a leading company providing resources for the world's business and investment leaders, providing them with commentary, analyses, relevant tools, and real-time reporting., including real-time original reporting on business, technology, investing, and lifestyle

The weekly *Forbes* magazine is also available online and whilst mainly designed for a US audience is read on a global basis. *Forbes* often carries articles and commentaries on entrepreneurs and entrepreneurial activities.

Other linked products from Forbes include:

» *Forbes Global*, covering the rise of capitalism around the world for international business leaders. Contains sections on Companies & Industry, Capital Markets & Investing, Entrepreneurs, Technology and Forbes Global Life.

Forbes newsletters include the following.

» *Forbes Aggressive Growth Investor*, a monthly newsletter recommending the 50 best growth and momentum stocks to own now as determined by a proprietary multi-dimensional computer analysis of over 3000 stocks.

- *Gilder Technology Report*, covering the smartest, most profitable way to invest in technology. Buy tomorrow's biggest technology winners today when their shares are cheap and you can potentially multiply your wealth 10 to 100 times. The *Gilder Technology Report* will show you how.
- *Special Situation Survey* with monthly stock recommendations - hold or sell advice on each recommendation and special investment reports.
- *New Economy Watch*, a newsletter that looks at Internet-based companies.

Harvard Business Review

The leading business and management resource. It is read world-wide and features contributions by the leading names in business and management. Published 10 times per annum and available by subscription. Linked to the world-renowned Harvard Business School.

Management Today

From the Institute of Management in the UK, monthly to members or by subscription. Often contains useful articles on issues concerning entrepreneurship together with a regular feature on the subject.

The Economist

Weekly current affairs magazine with a global approach. *The Economist* carries general current affairs news in addition to analyses and market news on a global basis. Issued both as a print version and online. Available by subscription or from newsstands.

Time

Time Magazine, whilst originally a US product, has a global readership and is one of the most important current affairs and commentary magazines in existence. To appear on the cover of *Time* is to have made it; to be the *Time* man/woman of the year is a considerable honor indeed.

Time covers a huge range of issues and is thus useful to the entrepreneurial organization as a source of material for the SPECTACLES/SWOT analyses covered in Chapter 5.

The print version is available either on subscription or from newsstands.

Time was the first news magazine to publish online, beginning in 1993, and launched TIME.com in 1994. According to Nielsen NetRatings, TIME.com is the most trafficked news magazine site online. It draws over five million visits per month and receives over 32 million monthly page views. The site covers the events impacting the world each day and offers its own perspective on the latest news. There are also sections entitled: Nation, Education, World, and Health.

LIFEmag.com looks at the defining moments and great events of our lives through photography. The site features a Picture of the Day, This Day in LIFE, and a searchable magazine and cover collection dating back to 1936.

ONmagazine.com is the online complement to ON, the monthly personal-tech magazine with million-plus sales from the editors of *Time*. The site is a before-you-buy authority on new gadgets and Web services. ONmagazine.com features a new hands-on review every weekday, along with jargon-free how-to-buy guides for popular product categories.

Wall Street Journal

A US financial daily carrying analysis, financial, and other commercial news plus company results. Available on subscription or from newsstands.

WEBSITES

www.business2.com	*Business 2* Website
www.easyJet.com	easyJet Website
www.economist.com	*The Economist* Website
www.forbes.com	Forbes Website
www.ft.com	*Financial Times* Website
www.hbsp.harvard.edu/products/hbr	*Harvard Business Review* Website

www.inst-mgt.org.uk	Institute of Management Website
www.microsoft.com	Microsoft Website
www.nokia.com	Nokia Website
www.time.com	*Time Magazine* Website
www.tompeters.com	Tom Peters's Website
www.wsj.com	*Wall Street Journal* Website

Ten Steps to Making the Entrepreneurial Organization Work

The 10 steps to a successful entrepreneurial organization are not difficult but they do require faith, vision, discipline, and a willingness to analyze the environment and take calculated risks. They are in summary:

1. Belief in the organization
2. Vision
3. Know the customer
4. Analyze the environment
5. Understand the organization
6. Calculate the risks
7. Tolerate failure and learn from it
8. Value the people and make it fun
9. Accept routines and those who carry them out
10. Know when to hold them, know when to fold them, know when to walk away, and know when to run.

Throughout this material it has been stressed that the entrepreneurial organization is not a new phenomenon but one that has been in existence since humans first began to trade with humans. There has always been somebody who has been faster to the market than a competitor and who has seen possibilities earlier than his or her counterparts

There is no luck attached to the entrepreneurial organization any more than the success of individual entrepreneurs can be ascribed to luck. Success to these organizations and individuals is a matter of carefully analyzing the external environment, assessing the markets, knowing their own strengths and weaknesses coupled to a willingness to take calculated risks, and all driven forward by vision.

It has also been shown that the non-entrepreneurial person has a role to play in an entrepreneurial organization, as there are many routine tasks that must be carried out to the same degree of efficiency etc. as the more entrepreneurial ones if the organization is to be successful. All of the entrepreneurial organizations covered in this material undertake routine tasks to the same high standards as entrepreneurial ones; their bills are paid on time, maintenance is carried out, supplies are ordered, and all to a consistent standard.

Luck plays a very small part in the entrepreneurial organization. As Peter Drucker (see Chapter 8) has pointed out, such organizations have a disciplined approach. The way they operate may be different to the methods used by less entrepreneurial organizations but they analyze the situation and only take those risks that they can afford and which they believe are likely to pay off. Most of all they know their customers.

The 10 steps listed below are those that an organization needs to take if it is to become entrepreneurial. Perhaps the first is the most important - the organization must believe in itself and its customers. It is not enough to be the best; the organization must believe that it is the best.

BELIEF IN THE ORGANIZATION

Without a belief in the organization, its products, services, and indeed its whole philosophy entrepreneurship will be difficult if not impossible. Peters and Waterman stressed the importance of excellent organizations believing that they were the best in *In Search of Excellence*. With such a belief comes pride and a wish by individuals to see the whole organization move forward. Whilst monetary gain may be part of the reason for this, as Herzberg showed, recognition and achievement are very important motivators. Entrepreneurial organizations do not just talk about excellence and quality - they deliver it in a consistent manner.

In the companion ExpressExec publication, *The Entrepreneurial Individual*, it is stressed that monetary gain is often not the prime motivator for such individuals. Many of them continue with their entrepreneurial activities long after they have all the money they could need, as shown by Bill Gates and Sir Richard Branson.

VISION

It is difficult for an organization to move forward if those in charge of it do not have a clear idea of the direction in which they wish it to move. Vision is a key requirement for an entrepreneurial organization because all progress will stem from and contribute to the fulfillment of the vision.

In many entrepreneurial organizations the vision is the product of the founder of the organization and it is imperative that it is communicated to all layers of the organization as clearly and as succinctly as possible. Many organizations now provide a card with the vision or mission statement printed on it for staff to carry with them.

Within the concept of vision those in charge of an entrepreneurial organization need to remember that their staff are human and that objectives whilst relating to the vision are also manageable. The C-SMART concept (Cartwright, 2000) that objectives should always be:

» customer centered
» specific
» measurable
» agreed
» realistic, and
» timely

should always be kept in mind. Giving people attainable objectives may slow a process down a little but is much more likely to result in success than giving a person a task that is almost impossible for them. Such an approach is usually frustrating and likely to end in full or partial failure.

KNOW THE CUSTOMER

Ultimately the success of any organization lies in the hands of its customers. It has become an axiom of modern business that it is no longer enough to satisfy customers; to retain them they must be delighted. Repeat business is for many organizations (one can exclude the police, prisons, and even some health provision from this statement as they will be deemed successful if they do not have repeat business) the major performance criterion.

To the entrepreneurial organization the customer is a valuable source of information and a marketing tool in that customers can recommend the organization to their friends, colleagues, and relatives. The customer is the partner in a relationship that will hopefully be a long and fruitful one.

The entrepreneurial organization spends a great deal of time getting to know the customer - becoming close to them. Even complaints may be welcomed by the entrepreneurial organization as more is learnt from what goes wrong than from what goes right. Entrepreneurial organizations should view complaints as an opportunity to strengthen the customer relationship by recovering the situation with alacrity.

ANALYZE THE ENVIRONMENT

The entrepreneurial organization knows its external environment. A great deal of time will be spent analyzing and monitoring the components of the SPECTACLES analysis introduced in Chapter 5. These factors, Social, Political, Economic, Cultural, Technological, Aesthetic, Customer, Legal, Environmental, and Sectoral, are the means by which the strengths and weaknesses of the organization are considered in respect of the opportunities and threats that the organization must exploit in terms of the former and defend against in terms of the latter.

Without understanding the external environment, an environment that may be more and more unfamiliar as the organization reaches out into the global marketplace, the best opportunities may be lost.

As the whole world becomes an opportunity due to the adoption of e-commerce, the more important an understanding of how different parts of the world and the associated markets behave becomes. Entrepreneurial organizations will also defend themselves against competition from other areas. If they can become global so can a competitor from somewhere else!

UNDERSTAND THE ORGANIZATION

All organizations have their strengths and weaknesses. Successful organizations do not try to pretend that they are perfect but recognize where improvements are needed and then implement policies and procedures to reduce any weaknesses.

The entrepreneurial organization, moving forward with growth strategies as it does, may, like an advancing army, be very vulnerable to weaknesses on its flanks.

One area where the entrepreneurial organization may be vulnerable is in its administration and routines (see below). These are the less glamorous aspects of organizational life and it takes discipline to ensure that the organization ensures that they receive as much attention and commitment as the more exciting entrepreneurial activities.

The organization should spend some time at least once or twice a year reflecting on what it is good at but also what is not being done as well as it could and who is affected. If it is the customer, then there are problems ahead.

CALCULATE THE RISKS

No organization can survive if it takes risks that are beyond its resources to survive if failure results.

Entrepreneurial organizations are willing to take risks but only after all the factors (external and internal - see above) have been calculated and the prospects for success weighed against the cost of failure.

The case of Virgin Atlantic quoted in Chapter 6 is a case in point. A risk of £2 million was a small one for Virgin. It might have been a large one for another organization and not worth taking. In Virgin's case, step 1 above certainly applied. Sir Richard Branson believes in himself, his organization, and its products!

Risks should be taken but not if they endanger the survival of the organization and they should only be taken after very careful analysis.

TOLERATE FAILURE AND LEARN FROM IT

Any organization that is prepared to take risks will eventually encounter a failure. If the organization has taken step 6 into account its survival will not be threatened, but the experience is likely to be uncomfortable.

When failure occurs it is all too easy to allocate blame. If the failure is due to incompetence, stupidity, or negligence then it may well be right that blame is allocated and somebody punished. It is important, however, to find out just who was to blame. For instance, if the failure was caused by a junior employee who had not been provided with sufficient resources, who is really to blame? Is it the employee or his or her supervisor?

The entrepreneurial organization relies on people "pushing the envelope" (a term that comes from testing the so-called flight envelope for new aircraft) and as such honest mistakes need to be tolerated if people are not to become so scared of punishment that they will no longer work at the edge.

Failures should always be investigated and analyzed, not to see who was to blame but to find out why it happened, what can be changed, and what lessons are there to be learnt.

VALUE THE PEOPLE AND MAKE IT FUN

No matter how entrepreneurial the senior management are or how good the products or how up to date the plant, in the end all organizations rely on the skill and attitudes of their people.

People come to work, in the main to earn money. However, they will be more productive and loyal if they receive recognition for their skills and enjoy what they are doing. Fun is not incompatible with work – it can be an integral part of it. If pride in one's work is encouraged and nurtured then a job well done is an enjoyable one.

Entrepreneurial organizations can be great fun to be in as so much is often happening. They can also be frustrating and a little scary. How secure are jobs etc.? The organization should ensure that everybody knows what is happening, that success is celebrated, and that all who contribute (however mundane their role) should be included in the celebrations.

ACCEPT ROUTINES AND THOSE WHO CARRY THEM OUT

As has been stressed throughout this material, the entrepreneurial organization has to carry out routine administration etc. alongside its more glamorous activities. The organization should never allow a "them and us" attitude to develop between groups of staff engaged in the two very different areas. Administration supports the entrepreneurial work and those carrying it out are just as valuable as anybody else is.

KNOW WHEN TO HOLD THEM, KNOW WHEN TO FOLD THEM, KNOW WHEN TO WALK AWAY, AND KNOW WHEN TO RUN

The final step is taken from a song entitled "The Gambler," recorded by Kenny Rodgers and written by D. Schiltz. The entrepreneurial organization knows when to move forward, knows which markets it should not enter, and it recognizes a dog (see Boston matrix) when it sees one and divests itself of it.

The entrepreneurial organization is above all else proactive. It leads and makes the running. We all depend on these organizations for progress, for without them the world would be a very different place.

KEY LEARNING POINTS

Any organization can become entrepreneurial but as a very minimum it must:

» Communicate its vision to all its staff.
» Value every member of staff.
» Be close to the customer.
» Understand itself and its environment.
» Tolerate and learn from failure.
» Take calculated risks.

Frequently Asked Questions (FAQs)

Q1: What is an entrepreneurial organization?

A: An entrepreneurial organization is one that is concerned with growth, is proactive rather than reactive, customer focused, can assess the risks involved in a venture and then take risks that seem likely to bring sustained growth and market share, is prepared to tolerate failure, and, lastly, has a large number of employees who share the vision and believe in the organization. You can read more about this in Chapters 2–7.

Q2: Can people who are not entrepreneurial fit into an entrepreneurial organization?

A: There are many routine tasks to be carried out in even the most thrusting entrepreneurial organization. These often need people with a methodical, attention to detail, type of mind. The important aspect for the organization is to have the right balance of people carrying out the tasks for which they are best suited. This issue is covered in Chapters 2 and 6.

Q3: Is an entrepreneurial organization always driven by a single personality?

A: Not always (British Airways in the 1990s is a good example of corporate entrepreneurship), but many entrepreneurial organizations because of their position within the organizational life cycle still have their founder or somebody close to that person at their head and that person often retains a great deal of power and influence over decision making. You can read more about this in Chapters 2, 6, and 7.

Q4: What type of culture characterizes an entrepreneurial organization?

A: Entrepreneurial organizations can often be shown as a spider's web (coined a power or club culture by Charles Handy). Power emanates from the center, as does much of the decision making. You can read more about culture in Chapter 5.

Q5: How has modern information and communications technology (ICT) aided the entrepreneurial organization?

A: ICT has provided new opportunities and markets for entrepreneurial organizations to supply with the materials (hardware, software, and consumables) required and has also enabled business to be carried out in a different manner as described in Chapter 4.

Q6: How important is the leader to an entrepreneurial organization?

A: Of critical importance. It is the leader who holds the vision and sets the tone for the whole organization. This is covered in more detail in Chapter 6.

Q7: Should organizations take risks?

A: If they want to move forward they have to. Nothing about the future is certain. The entrepreneurial organization takes calculated risks based on a careful analysis of the external and internal factors identified as being of key importance. There is more detail on this issue in Chapters 1, 2, 5, 6, and 7.

Q8: If something goes wrong, shouldn't somebody be blamed?

A: If they are incompetent, negligent, or stupid - yes. If they were not provided with the resources they needed, that is a different matter. If something goes wrong through an honest mistake then this is an opportunity for learning, not for punishment. This is covered in more detail in Chapter 6.

Q9: How important is the customer to the entrepreneurial organization?

A: Nobody is more important. Entrepreneurial organizations have very close relationships with their customers. After all, a decline in customers means less growth and no customers equals no business. This is covered in more detail in Chapters 2, 3, and 7.

Q10: Where are resources available to assist in understanding the entrepreneurial organization?

A: A list of books, journals, and Web addresses will be found in Chapter 9.

Index

Printed and bound in the UK by
CPI Antony Rowe, Eastbourne

Printed and bound by CPI Group (UK) Ltd, Croydon, CR0 4YY

13/04/2025

14656559-0002